Challenges Of Cultural And Racial Diversity To Counseling:

Volume 2

Latin America And The United States

Mexico City Conference Proceedings

Edited by:

Gerardo M. Gonzalez, PhD

Isaura Alvarado, PhD, NCC

Alberto S. Segrera, MA

Foreword by *Sunny Hansen, PhD, NCC, NCCC*
President, 1989–1990
American Association for Counseling and Development

A Note From the Publisher

This is a selected proceedings of the second international conference sponsored by ACA. Not all of the presenters are represented in this publication. Those papers included were intended as working drafts, and should be considered as such.

On July 1, 1992 the American Association for Counseling and Development (AACD) became the American Counseling Association (ACA).

Copyright © 1993 by the American Counseling Association

All rights reserved.

American Counseling Association
5999 Stevenson Avenue
Alexandria, VA 22304

Cover Design by Sarah Jane Valdez

Library of Congress Cataloging-in-Publication Data

Challenges from Latino/Hispanic cultures : Mexico City conference proceedings / edited by
  Gerardo M. Gonzalez, Isaura Alvarado, Alberto S. Segrera ; foreword by Sunny Hansen.
      p.   cm.
  Papers from the second international conference of the American Counseling Association
held in Mexico City, June 1990, in cooperation with the Latin-American Federation of
Associations and Professionals in Guidance.
  Includes bibliographical references.
  ISBN 1-55620-102-8
  1. Cross-cultural counseling—United States. 2. Hispanic Americans—
Psychology. I. Gonzalez, Gerardo M. II. Alvarado, Isaura. III. Segrera, Alberto S.
BF637.C6C367   1993
158′.3′08968—dc20   92-22752
                                                                              CIP

Printed in the United States of America

CONTENTS

FOREWORD

To further ACA's international and multicultural goals, the second International Conference was held in Mexico City in June 1990, with the cooperation of the Latin-American Federation of Associations and Professionals in Guidance (FAPOAL). The conference developed out of recognition of the tremendous growth of Latino/Hispanic populations in the United States and the need for counselors and human development specialists to be much more knowledgeable about and sensitive to diverse Latino/Hispanic cultures both within the United States and in Latin America.

The Mexico City conference was a fitting conclusion to a year in which AACD's theme was "Global Visions—Celebrating Diversity, Creating Community." Whereas the first AACD offshore conference was in London in 1989, this was the first in a country in which English is not the primary language. Unfortunately, due to budget constraints, the primary conference language was English, but volunteer interpreters and translators were utilized.

An Advisory Committee consisting of representatives from the Association for Multicultural Counseling and Development, the International Relations Committee, Latino/Hispanic leaders, and AACD staff planned the conference. Together they designed the 4-day meeting, including a diverse group of keynote speakers and workshop and paper presenters, along with cross-cultural working groups. Objectives of the conference, consistent with AACD values recognizing "the interconnectedness of individuals, organizations, and societies," were focused on the four themes of community, diversity, communication, and spirituality. The conference sought to:

1. Stimulate dialogue across cultures about counseling issues from a global perspective, focusing on Latino/Hispanic concerns;
2. Share current theory and practice in various cultures and the effects of political, social, economic, and spiritual influences on the delivery of counseling;
3. Explore values, conflicts, and the place of beliefs, traditions, and spirituality within and between cultures and between counselors and clients;
4. Examine specific counseling and social issues, skills, programs, and the approaches (including indigenous approaches) used to address them in each culture; and
5. Provide an understanding of the cultural context and unique counseling problems and strategies within Mexico, the host country.

Although the conference was intended to be bilateral between the United States and Mexico, about 150 participants from 18 countries attended the meeting, including Chile, Bolivia, Guam, Cuba, Puerto Rico, Uruguay, Spain, Japan, West Germany, Ecuador, Costa Rica, Venezuela, Argentina, and Brazil.

It is difficult if not impossible to capture the spirit or recapitulate the events of the conference, but a few observations will be made. Participants responded very positively to the plenary speakers, the working groups, and the papers/workshops. Data were provided on the diversity of Latino/Hispanics in the United States, and several speakers cited diversity in their own country. Participants were made aware of the "English Only" controversy in the United States and were introduced to the important idea of "English Plus," as well as language issues in other cultures. One speaker drew upon the concept of counselors as "healers" to explicate the importance of intercultural communication and exchange. A curandera, who has been a healer working with Latino/Hispanics in Colorado for many years, described her work and especially her collaboration with other mental health professionals. The importance of nonverbal communication in understanding culture was stressed in a spirited presentation. The theme of a vision for a more humane and less biased future was also presented.

To offer insights into Mexico's culture, field visits were scheduled to include the Pyramids, Ballet Folklorico, the Mariachi Center, local universities, and various cultural and historic centers in Mexico City. Opening and closing banquets with characteristic folk music added a festive atmosphere. Formal greetings were given by representatives from governments of the United States (Gerard Bowers) and Mexico (Rafael Fernandez de Castro), as well as by leaders of AACD and FAPOAL.

Generally it can be said that a good beginning was made in addressing the conference objectives. Overall evaluations were positive, and the atmosphere was described as friendly and productive. One participant remarked that "the ambiance and flavor were conducive to excellent networking" and another that "the conference will greatly impact my life." The conference succeeded in bringing together counselors from the United States, Mexico, and Latin countries to help each other understand issues of counseling Latino/Hispanic clients within and across national boundaries. The four themes were separate yet interrelated and provided a useful and timely basis for working group discussions. Respect for one another seemed to characterize the groups, led by experienced facilitators. It is evident also that the groups generated excellent interactions and recommendations for action in areas such as public policy, counseling research, counseling practice, and counselor preparation. Group summaries and recommendations are presented at the end of this volume.

Some important lessons also were learned from this conference. Perhaps the most important relate to the host country. It was unfortunate that the minimal conference budget did not allow for simultaneous translation of speeches into Spanish, as a number of Latinos were not fluent in English and most Americans were not fluent in Spanish; thus both missed out on considerable content. Because of the language difficulties in some of the working groups, some Spanish-speaking participants formed a separate working group—a situation that limited their interaction with other participants. Conference coordinators spontaneously organized one bilingual session in which papers, comments, and questions were translated into both English and Spanish. Although that process took much longer than the scheduled time, members appreciated the effort to improve intercultural communication. The fact that the AACD president gave a small part of her introductory and closing remarks in Spanish also was appreciated by the Spanish-speaking participants. In planning future conferences, attempts should be made to have simultaneous translation and/or interpreters available throughout the sessions.

Another lesson learned was that international conferences need to take into account the economy and incomes of counselors in the host country and other developing nations. Although counselors from the United States may be able to afford staying in an expensive hotel, the hotel costs were too high for many participants from Latin American countries. Also, there should have been more presentations from the host country. For a number of circumstantial reasons, the involvement of FAPOAL was not as great as the coordinators would have liked.

Nonetheless, despite these areas for improvement, the Mexico Conference was a success. And a number of persons contributed to that success. Although not all can be mentioned here, the Advisory Committee deserves a vote of thanks for helping identify speakers, reviewing proposals, and offering ideas in conceptualizing the conference. Special appreciation needs to be expressed to all the keynote speakers and workshop and paper presenters, who stimulated thought and discussion. The 10 working group leaders and recorders, organized by Bob Nejedlo, contributed a great deal by facilitating the discussions and documenting proceedings. The conference summarizers—Isaura Alvarado, Priscilla Chavez-Reilly, and Ricardo Blanco—pulled together the major ideas from the groups and made sense of them in their final report. Alberto Segrera was interpreter and translator par excellence and greatly enhanced communication for both English-speaking and Spanish-speaking participants. Letitia Rodriguez, president of FAPOAL, though unable to attend all of the conference, participated in the planning and brought leaders from her association, including Ricardo Blanco, who represented her.

Behind the scenes a number of AACD staff members worked to bring the Mexico Conference to reality. Patrick Christoff handled all of the hotel, travel, publicity, and program details, and Nancy Pinson-Millburn was extremely helpful in arranging speakers. Others attending from AACD staff were Acting Director William Hunter and Teresa Alfaro, Convention Assistant. AACD leaders participating were Past President Bob Nejedlo, President-Elect Jane Myers, ASCA President Doris Coy, and AMCD President Linda Torrence.

As for this monograph, if it were not for the AACD Media Committee, these proceedings would not have been published. Special appreciation is expressed to Richard Hayes and Loretta Bradley, former and present Media chairpersons, for their support. Current Associate Executive Director Mark Hamilton and Acquisitions and Development Editor Elaine Pirrone also were of great assistance. Finally, the greatest appreciation goes to our bilingual monograph editors, who generously agreed to take on this added responsibility—Gerardo Gonzalez, Lead Editor, University of Florida; Isaura Alvarado, Puerto Rico; and Alberto Segrera, Mexico.

From the inception of this conference, the committee hoped that a publication of some of the papers might be possible. We believed then as we do now that the ideas and recommendations presented deserved a wider audience than the 150 who were able to interact in Mexico. Our hope was that the themes would stimulate AACD members and our Latino counterparts to think about their work and their world in different ways—and to translate those thoughts into action. We knew that in Mexico and at this conference, we would be learners.

Experiences such as the Mexico Conference make us acutely aware of our commonalities as members of the human family dealing with common issues on an endangered planet—as well as of our differences and how sensitively we as professionals and as persons must deal with them both within and across cultures. In Mexico we were reminded that, despite the ills of the world, we are an optimistic profession. We believe that growth and development can occur, that individuals and societies can change, and that we as counselors can help shape those changes. We were reminded of the importance of being able to communicate—to understand and be understood—in another language. We learned that social interactions can break down many barriers, especially when people can eat, sing, dance, and laugh together. We hope that these proceedings help you to share a little of the flavor of the AACD Mexico Conference and to gain some knowledge, understanding, and insights about counseling Latino/Hispanic clients and stimulate you to want to learn more.

—Sunny Hansen, PhD, NCC, NCCC
Chair, Conference Advisory Committee
AACD President, 1989–1990

MEXICO CITY CONFERENCE

Planning and On-Site Coordinators

Conference Advisory Committee

Sunny Hansen   Edwin Herr
Nancy Pinson-Millburn   Letitia Rodriguez
Mario Rivas   Isaura Alvarado
Gerardo Gonzalez   Arthur Sanchez
Farah A. Ibrahim   Priscilla Chavez-Reilly

Conference Committee Members in Attendance

Isaura Alvarado   Gerardo Gonzalez
Priscilla Chavez-Reilly   Charlotte Rodriguez

Conference Summarizers

Carl Barham   Rita Robinson
Doris Coy   Charlotte Rodriguez
Elizabeth Gama   Alberto Segrera
Kevin Hennelly   Linda Torrence
Robert Nejedlo   Veronica Kaune-Wilde

Association Officials

AACD

Sunny Hansen   President
William Hunter   Acting Executive Director
Nancy Pinson-Millburn   Assistant Executive Director
                                       for Assoc. & Prof. Relations
Patrick Christoff   Director of Professional
                                       Development & Research

Mexico

Alberto Segrera   Universidad Iberoamericana, Mexico City

FAPOAL

Letitia Rodriquez   President
Ricardo Blanco   Representative

PREFACE

Global political and economic changes make it imperative that communication and cooperation among people of the world be enhanced. The North America Free Trade Agreement involving Canada, the United States, and Mexico and the cooperative anti-drug initiatives by the presidents of Bolivia, Peru, Colombia, Ecuador, and the United States are two recent examples of how the nations of North, Central, and South America are confronting the challenge of greater international cooperation for addressing important issues in the Americas. International economic, social, and political developments create special contexts for counseling and human development. Poverty, unemployment, women's rights, drugs, HIV infection and AIDS, and changing family structures are fertile areas for counselor interventions. Access to education and jobs and adequate health care also are universal issues across cultures.

In the United States, the Latino/Hispanic population is the fastest growing "minority" group. In the 1950s, about 50% of U.S. immigrants came from Europe. However, during the 1970s, only 18% came from Europe and more than 30% came from Latin America. These demographic changes are challenging the counseling profession in the United States to become more sensitive to Latin American culture as well as to the special needs of Latino/Hispanic populations throughout the Americas.

The mission of the conference in Mexico City in June 1990 was to bring together counselors and other human development specialists, including theorists and researchers, to examine the challenges posed by the increasingly diverse Spanish-speaking populations located throughout the Americas. An attempt was made to clarify the roles of helping professionals as mediators and advocates for persons of Latino/Hispanic origin, with particular attention to ethnic/cultural identification and within-group differences. An effort also was made to consider the contribution that indigenous practices make to counseling in Latin America and the social and economic consequences of majority-minority relations in both Latin American and North American cultures.

This conference promoted and facilitated important dialogue about the broad issues of community, diversity, communication, and spiritual concerns that affect Latino/Hispanic groups. Indeed, numerous presentations and discussions focused on each of these broad topics; thus, this monograph is organized around these four areas of emphasis. Each section includes a plenary session paper and others representative of those presented at the conference. Because of the overlap among these topics and space limitations, we had to make some arbitrary decisions about which papers to include. However, a listing of all the papers presented at the conference and their authors is included at the end of this monograph for those who wish to obtain additional information. Also included is a list of recommendations conference participants made regarding public policy, counseling research, counselor preparation, and counseling practice. We and the conference organizers believe that these proceedings and recommendations provide meaningful insight into Latin American culture, issues, and concerns. We hope this monograph will form the basis for further development of an international, action-oriented counseling and human development agenda focused on Latino/Hispanic populations. We dedicate this monograph to that end.

—Gerardo M. Gonzalez, PhD
University of Florida, Gainesville

—Isaura Alvarado, PhD, NCC
University of Puerto Rico, San Juan

—Alberto S. Segrera, MA
Universidad Iberoamericana, Mexico

PART I

COMMUNITY

Establishing a sense of community is central to the well-being and positive development of immigrant and other minority groups. Such things as a common language, traditions, religion, family orientation, work ethic, and values enhance the sense of community among Latino/Hispanic groups. More so than the traditional social institutions, it is the community that has historically provided the necessary support and assistance to help Latino/Hispanics cope with adversity. Based on a culture of mutual support and concern for the common good, Latino/Hispanic groups often place community above self-interest. Thus, feeling connected to their community is one of the most important sources of identity for Latino/Hispanic individuals.

In part 1, the presenters address the centrality of a sense of community to Latino/Hispanic identity and lifestyle. In the plenary session Amado Padilla discusses the English Only movement in the United States, and the threat it presents to the Latino/Hispanic culture's sense of community. In the first paper, Mary Brabeck discusses the conceptions of self that emerged from her interviews of young men in the Guatemalan highlands, and how such conceptions are intricately related to a sense of community. Finally, Pedro Sanchez, Dorothy Soukup, and Silvia Pech Campos present results of their research comparing career development values of 15-year-olds from Mexico and the United States.

PLENARY ADDRESS

MYTHS, REALITIES, AND IMPLICATIONS OF THE ENGLISH ONLY MOVEMENT IN THE UNITED STATES

Amado M. Padilla

Abstract

The author discusses the recent efforts undertaken in the United States to make English the official national language. He argues that this English Only movement, as the effort is known, has connections to restrictionist anti-immigration organizations with powerful and heavily funded political influence. The major implications of this movement for social/psychological development, education, psychological assessment, and the delivery of human services to Latino/Hispanic groups are presented. Research shows that positive self- and ethnic identification occurs best when children are allowed access to both their heritage language and English. Furthermore, it is argued that the English Only movement is potentially detrimental to the few gains made in the past two decades to develop culturally sensitive assessment techniques and human services systems for Latinos.

Resumen

El autor discute los esfuerzos recientes emprendidos en los Estados Unidos para hacer el inglés la lengua oficial de la nación. El mantiene que este movimiento únicamente de inglés, como se conoce el esfuerzo, tiene relaciones con organizaciones restrictivas de antiinmigración las cuales tienen una influencia poderosa y política de profundos fondos. Se presentan las implicaciones principales de este movimiento para el desarrollo social/psicológico, la educación, la valoración psicológica, y la entrega de servicios humanos a los grupos latinohispánicos. Además, se mantiene que el movimiento únicamente de inglés es potencialmente perjudicial a las pocas ganancias que se han hecho en los últimos dos decenios para desarrollar técnicas de valoración y sistemas de servicios humanos culturalmente sensibles para los latinos. La investigación enseña que la identificación de sí étnica positiva mejor sucede cuando se permiten a los niños el acceso a su lengua de herencia tanto como al inglés.

Introduction

We are bound to our language as members of society, as members of communities, and through a set of professional values and responsibilities. Language is central to culture, and language is what binds communities of people together. This topic promises to be interesting, intellectually stimulating, provocative, and professionally challenging. My discussion focuses on the English Only movement in the United States and on the myths, realities, and implications that this movement has on both ethnic and professional communities.

In recent years there has been considerable attention and debate about whether English should be designated as the official language of the United States. Organized movements such as U.S. English and English First have as their primary purpose to make English the official language of the United States. This is to be accomplished either through an amendment to the U.S. Constitution, through state legislation, or through repeal of laws and regulations permitting public business to be conducted in a language other than English.

To date, 18 states have enacted laws designating English as the official state language. These states are Alabama, Arizona, Arkansas, California, Colorado, Florida, Georgia, Hawaii, Illinois, Indiana, Kentucky, Mississippi, Nebraska, North Carolina, North Dakota, South Carolina, Tennessee, and Virginia. It is important to point out that a federal district judge in Arizona has declared that the Arizona constitutional amendment making English the official language of all governmental functions is a violation of the federally protected free speech act. In addition, Hawaii has not one but two official languages—English and Hawaiian.

As various states have considered constitutional amendments making English the official language, legal scholars (Piatt, 1990) have been examining the constitutional provisions that apply to language rights as used in the classroom, workplace, courtroom, and social service agency. The fervor of interest and diversity of opinion given to language issues was matched only once before—at the turn of the century. Then, however, language issues were confined to local or state arenas, whereas today the initiatives dedicated to establishing English as the official language are being orchestrated at the national level by powerful and heavily funded political organizations. Furthermore, the English Only movement has close connections to restrictionist anti-immigration organizations, which suggests that this movement has a wider, more far-reaching, and more negative agenda than simply advocating an English Only policy. For example, until mid-1988, U.S. English was a project of an organization called U.S. Incorporated, a tax-exempt corporation that also supports the Federation of American Reform, Americans for Border Control, Californians for Population Stabilization, and other immigration restrictionist groups.

It is important to clarify the misconceptions surrounding the English Only efforts and to demonstrate the relevance of this movement to professionals such as ourselves. This presentation is organized into four major sections that correspond to the areas most affected by the English Only movement. These are social/psychological issues, educational issues, issues affecting testing, and issues affecting health service delivery.

Social/Psychological Issues

English Only advocates argue that a national policy declaring English as the official language of the United States is essential because without such a policy the country risks being balkanized by non-English language groups. The case of Canada and the French-speaking community in Quebec is frequently cited as an example of what might happen in the United States if an official language policy is not adopted. In Quebec the French Canadians have instituted a policy of linguistic determinism that recognizes the legitimacy of French in all sectors of public life. That is, French has replaced English as the mode of communication in business, provision of services, and education in the province. Opponents of English Only have been quick to counter that the circumstances in Canada and the United States are not equivalent and that parallels cannot be drawn between the two countries in establishing U.S. language policy. For example, there are significant historical differences between the French-speaking community in Canada and the indigenous language and linguistic minority communities in the United States. In addition, power relationships between the Canadian French-speaking and English-speaking communities are strikingly different from those between the dominant White and linguistic minority groups, especially Hispanics, in the United States. More importantly, though, four significant issues invalidate the English Only position here. The first issue addresses the willingness to shift from the native language to English. The second issue focuses on racist attitudes that seem to underlie English Only. The third issue pertains to interethnic group relations, and the fourth to the role language plays in social and ethnic identity.

Language Shifts

One of the arguments that has been used repeatedly by English Only advocates is that some linguistic minority groups, most notably Hispanics, and to a lesser extent Asian Americans, are resistant to surrendering the use of their native language following immigration to the United States, and that only a national language policy would ensure a language shift to English. In contrast, however, immigrants clearly recognize the importance of learning English as a way of improving their socioeconomic and geographic mobility in the United States, as illustrated by the following quotes: "If my language problem could be solved, everything would be better;" "Life is hard for me because I can't read or write in English;" "Since I don't know English, I find myself a dumb and blind person in this society." Thus, immigrants repeatedly express their need to learn English, contrary to what English Only advocates claim. Several studies show that language shifts occur generally within one or two generations, again, contrary to what the English Only position suggests. On the basis of these data, some English Only opponents hold that it is the non-English languages of immigrants that are in danger of extinction, not English.

Racism

If the non-English languages are not maintained, contrary to what the English Only advocates claim, then what is the motive for people who advocate an English Only position? Crawford (1989) and a number of other scholars who have examined this issue suggest that racist attitudes seem to be behind English Only initiatives. It is now generally well known, for example, that Linda Chavez, the one-time Hispanic director of U.S. English, resigned her position in late 1988, after an inflammatory racist memo authored by John Tanton, Chairman of U.S. English, was made public. In his document,

Tanton listed a range of cultural threats posed by Spanish-speaking immigrants. Among the threats he identified were the following: "The tradition of the mordida (bribe), the lack of involvement in public affairs, Roman Catholicism with its potential to 'pitch out the separation of church and state,' the low educability and high school-dropout rate, failure to use birth control, limited concern for the environment, and, of course, language divisions" (Crawford, p. 57).

For these and other reasons in the memo, the English Only advocates claim that a national policy for English must be ensured. After this memo was released, not only did Linda Chavez resign, but Walter Cronkite, who was on the Board of Advisors for English Only, also resigned in protest. The belief that English Only may appeal to racist beliefs is also illustrated by a study of letters to the editor in newspapers around the country in support of English Only. One interesting study analyzed the letters to the editor that appeared in California newspapers in 1986, when Proposition 63, which would make English the official language of California, was before the voters. The study indicated the presence of very strong racist attitudes behind English Only. In fact, the publisher and health advocate, Norman Cousins, who also was on the Board of Advisors for English Only, resigned to protest the negative symbolic significance of Proposition 63—the English Only amendment to the California constitution. Cousins explained his resignation by stating that if English Only continued at the rate at which it was going, it would cause language minority citizens to be "disadvantaged, denigrated, and demeaned." An example of this denigration and demeaning can be found in a number of communities like Monterey Park in California, where Asian language books were removed from the library shelves and banned from libraries after Proposition 63 was passed. In other locales there have been bans designed to limit commerce in languages other than English. Employees have also been fired because of the use of non-English languages in the workplace. For instance, a Philippino hospital worker in Pomona, California, was fired because she was speaking Tagalo, and in Miami cashiers have been fired because they were speaking Spanish on the job.

Intergroup Relations

Over the past decade there have been sharp increases in the number of hate crimes and other forms of antiminority group sentiment. We have seen an increase in Ku Klux Klan demonstrations. Neo-Nazi activists and young skinheads attempt to intimidate individuals because of differences in race, ethnicity, religion, or sexual orientation. So commonplace have these events become that in 1990 the U.S. Congress and President Bush signed into law a bill to, for the first time ever, keep statistics on hate crimes.

We have known for a long time that the more favorably one's own group is perceived, the less attractive other groups are viewed. This makes ethnocentrism the psychological mechanism that promotes in-group/out-group cleavage and prejudice of all kinds. The English Only movement and the arguments its advocates use to justify their actions are similar to those used at other times and places to force one group's domination of another.

Social and Ethnic Identification

The process of an individual's identification with a group is an issue of considerable significance to developmental psychology and counseling. Although the area of identity development in language minority students is an important issue, it has not received much empirical inquiry. However, several lines of research show that the position advocated by English Only in requiring a child or adolescent to give up his or her native language for the acquisition of English holds more implications at a personal level than merely the subtraction of the native language from an individual's linguistic repertoire. The reason for this belief lies in the close linkage between language and identification. As Ferdman (1990) recently pointed out in the *Harvard Educational Review*, "For Puerto Ricans in the U.S., the Spanish language is not just a means of communication, it also represents their identification as Latinos." When an immigrant attempts to lose all traces of his or her native language and culture, the result may be disastrous because the person has no real feeling of identity with the host culture to replace the original culture, which leads to the undesirable condition of cultural marginality.

Richard Rodriguez (1982) clearly demonstrated the significance of this point in his autobiography, *Hunger of Memory*, in which he described the turning point in his language background when nuns from a Catholic school visited his parents at home and encouraged them strongly to switch to English with their children. Rodriguez described the effects of the language shift on the family's interaction at home:

> The family's quiet was partly due to the fact that, as we children learned more and more English we shared fewer and fewer words with our parents. Sentences needed to be spoken slowly when a child addressed his mother or father. Often the parent wouldn't understand. The child would need to repeat. Still the parent misunderstood. The young voice, frustrated, would end by saying: never mind. The subject was closed. Dinners would be noisy with a clinking of knives and forks against the dishes. (p. 23)

In short, the psychological consequences can be enormous for people involved in any form of subtractive language shift because attitudes toward their own group, themselves, and society are seriously affected. Thus, the subtractive language policies advocated by English Only can have detrimental effects on children's identification with their cultural group, their self-concept, and U.S. society in general.

Bilingual Education

A few comments about the implications of English Only on education follow, primarily about issues having to do with bilingual education and its effectiveness. To understand the significant impact of the English Only movement on the education of linguistic minority students requires a slight digression to demographics. The U.S. Department of Education has concluded that somewhere between 1.1 and 2.6 million children in U.S. schools require instruction in English as a second language. This number is terribly inaccurate. It is known, for instance, that in 1989 the official number of students with limited proficiency in English in California alone was 740,000. Therefore, the actual number is probably much larger for the United States as a whole. About 75% of all such students in the United States are Hispanic or Latino. Thus, the English Only movement, which directs much of its resources against bilingual education, is primarily directing them at linguistic minority students who happen to be primarily Latino. English Only advocates and other opponents of bilingual education have voraciously disparaged the ineffectiveness of bilingual education for language minority children. As Crawford and others pointed out, critics of bilingual education have had an edge in the controversy over its effectiveness. Where evidence is contradictory, the easiest position to defend and the hardest to disprove is that results are inconclusive. The U.S. Department of Education requests proof that bilingual education is universally effective with every limited-English-proficient child, from every background, in every school. This is a standard that has been set for no other program funded by the U.S. Department of Education. In other words, the criteria for effectiveness of bilingual education are much more stringent than for any other program funded by the federal government through its education office, demonstrating a policy shift against bilingual education. Consequently, fewer than 20% of all limited-English-proficient students in the United States are enrolled in bilingual education programs. As a result, most of the children who have limited proficiency in English and are in need of English language instruction are not receiving a bilingual education. In sum, the argument that bilingual education is ineffective is only a paper tiger, and the motives have more to do with politics than educational pedagogy per se.

Psychological Assessment

Our third topic has to do with testing issues. It is known that the use of intelligence and achievement instruments plays an important role in special education, especially in the identification and placement of children. Yet there is a policy and scientific debate about the validity of intelligence and achievement tests for assessing bilingual children. There is a consensus among school psychologists and special education practitioners that language minority children's school achievement may be seriously underestimated if testing is conducted only in English. Indeed, existing national policy under the provision of Public Law 94–142 requires that ability testing be done in a manner sensitive to students' linguistic and cultural background. Federal law and most state special education policies promote the use of non-English and bilingual ability testing and culturally sensitive test interpretation where indicated. However, testing practices do not meet these criteria very well. Significant criticisms beyond the failure to consider non-English testing or bilingual testing include inappropriate construction and equating of translated tests, lack of reliability and validity studies, failure to develop testing performance norms for language minority student populations, and failure to use test administrators who are familiar with the language and cultural characteristics of the children tested. These concerns have arisen within the special education field per se, but they aptly summarize the key provisions and principles for testing language minority students at any educational level. For example, the current Standards for Educational and Psychological Testing were developed jointly by the American Psychological Association, the American Education Research Association, and the National Council on Measurement in Education. It is clear that special education policies and professional standards for conducting testing at all educational levels are inconsistent with views emanating from the English Only perspective. Professional policies and standards view familiarity with a non-English language as a resource that contributes to children's cognitive and academic functioning.

Taking English Only to its logical extreme would suggest that everything has to be done in English, and that is the direction in which that movement is flowing. On the other hand, we have Public Law 92–142, which states that testing has to be sensitive to the child being tested, and the standards manuals that require testing to be sensitive linguistically and culturally. Evidently there is a growing inconsistency between what the federal laws and professional practice require regarding linguistic minority children and what the English Only movement hopes to accomplish. Anyone engaged in psychometric assessment of linguistic minority children where the testing is done solely in English is in violation not only of the professional standards that we have set for ourselves through our major professional associations, but also in violation of certain federal laws. Yet, English Only advocates would argue that these "best" practices are wrong and assessment should be carried out in English only.

Providing Human Services

Another concern regarding an English Only policy is what it might mean in regard to the provision of human services to limited-English-speaking clients. For example, in California, the English Only amendment maintains that public services should be provided in English, except in the case of emergencies. However, there is underrepresentation of ethnic minority health care providers, or providers with bilingual skills, to supply these emergency services. As a consequence, an English Only policy might reduce even further the delivery of extremely limited general medical, mental health, and other social services to many Americans not proficient in English who may not know how to access human services or realize their right to seek such services despite their language barrier. If there are no health practitioners who can provide services in the clients' language, it is much easier to fall back on the provision of English Only and conclude that such provision is not required. Tension about this issue is growing and will continue to grow in the 1990s.

Now let me summarize some of the reasons why the relationship between language and human services is crucial. We know, for instance, that physicians who speak only English establish significantly better rapport with English-speaking patients than they do with Spanish-speaking patients. One study showed that English-speaking patients were given a better explanation of their therapeutic regimen than were Spanish-speaking patients, and physicians were able to elicit patient feedback significantly better from English-speaking patients than from Spanish-speaking patients (Shapiro & Saltzer, 1981).

In a related study, Manson (1988) examined the effects of language concordance between the physician and patient as a determinant of patient compliance. The findings indicated that the language discordant group was more likely than the language concordant group to be noncompliant in regard to their medication. Moreover, patients in the language discordant group were more likely to miss an appointment and were more likely to make emergency room visits.

Examining the health care literature with respect to Latinos in the United States shows that physicians, mental health practitioners, and other social service providers assert that Latinos don't keep appointments and that Latinos make one or two appointments and then don't return. The literature is beginning to show quite clearly, though, that the reason for this is the discordance between a monolingual English health provider and an individual whose language facility is greater in a non-English language. For example, physicians and other health care providers often talk about patient noncompliance. Latinos are noncompliant. Research shows, however, that they are noncompliant probably because they don't understand completely the instructions and advice of the health care providers.

In the area of mental health, Marcos, Alpert, Urcuyo, and Kesselman (1973) found that Hispanics show more psychopathology in their weaker language than in their stronger language. Even if the clients are bilingual and are treated in English, which is their weaker language, they will seem to be more disorganized and more schizo-phrenic, resulting in a more negative diagnostic evaluation than justified because of miscommunications when using English. Even if the bilingual clients are strongly pro-ficient in English, often the experiences they have to relate occurred when they were in a Spanish environment and have to be related in English. As a result the clients cannot relate these experiences as clearly as they would like. If you have an emotional experience in one language it is difficult to express it in a different language. English Only advocates consider all these issues surrounding bilingual services, compliance, and misdiagnosis irrelevant because they feel that English should be the only language used in the public sector.

Conclusions

Based on a review of scientific literature, there is no basis to justify the English Only position. For instance, research on language shift has shown that all ethnolinguistic groups, including Hispanics, demonstrate a shift in their expressive language prefer-ence from the home language to English, usually in one generation. In fact, opponents of English Only have always argued strongly that English language proficiency is es-sential and can be achieved without denial of the heritage language.

The leadership of the English Only movement promotes racist and anti-immigra-tion sentiment, and this is most likely the element that motivates, at least in part, supporters of the English Only initiative. Evidence shows that intergroup cooperation can be developed in an atmosphere that fosters linguistic pluralism. Positive self- and ethnic identification occurs when children are allowed access to both their heritage language and English.

A charge made in support of English Only is that bilingual education is an inef-fective method of instruction and that it maintains linguistic minority students in a position where they neither learn English nor aspire toward educational and social integration. A careful review of the major current studies in the area of bilingual education indicates that bilingual education is an effective educational technique for bridging the gap between a non-English home language and English in the school. Moreover, when bilingual education is implemented in a context that fosters a positive attitude toward bilingualism, then marked changes in school achievement, self-esteem, and intergroup cooperation are observed.

It is clear that specific educational policies as expressed in Public Law 94–142 and in professional standards for testing at all levels, as stated in the Standards for Edu-cational and Psychological Testing, are inconsistent with views emanating from the English Only perspective. Unlike the English Only perspective, these policies advocate testing linguistic minority individuals in ways that are sensitive to the strengths of their non-English language background. In addition, it is generally acknowledged today by psycholinguists that proficiency in two languages contributes to children's cognitive and academic functioning. Strategies that access the facilitatory role of bilingualism in children's school accomplishments are called for in our reevaluation of the testing of linguistic minority children.

Language considerations are also important in the delivery of health and mental health services. Ample evidence, for example, shows that diagnosis, treatment, and patient compliance can all be affected by whether the health care provider is able to communicate in the patient's native language. Accordingly, these practical considerations merit our increased attention to the service delivery needs of linguistic minority clients, rather than to the policies for curtailing such services as advocated by English Only supporters.

References

Crawford, J. (1989). *Bilingual education: History, politics, theory and practice*. Trenton, NJ: Crane.

Ferdman, B. M. (1990). Literacy and cultural identity. *Harvard Educational Review, 60,* 181, 204.

Manson, A. (1988). Language concordance as a determinant of patient compliance and emergency room visits in patients with asthma. *Medical Care, 26,* 1119–1128.

Marcos, L. R., Alpert, M., Urcuyo, L., & Kesselman, M. (1973). The effect of interview language on the evaluation of psychopathology in Spanish-American schizophrenic patients. *American Journal of Psychiatry, 130,* 549–553.

Piatt, B. (1990). *Only English: Law and language policy in the United States*. Albuquerque, NM: University of New Mexico Press.

Rodriguez, R. (1982). *Hunger of memory: The education of Richard Rodriquez*. New York: Bantam Books.

Shapiro, J., & Saltzer, E. (1981, December). Cross-cultural aspects of physician-patient communication patterns. *Urban Health, 10,* 10–15.

Models of Self Among Young Men in the Guatemalan Highlands

Mary M. Brabeck

Abstract

In this paper the author proposes two models of self and associated cultural values that have been proposed in recent psychological theory. She presents the findings of an examination of these conceptions of self in interviews she conducted in Guatemala with 40 indigenous and Ladino male adolescents. The implications of this work for mental health workers are discussed, and suggestions for the improvement of services to this population are made.

Resumen

En este artículo la autora propone dos modelos del yo y los valores culturales asociados que se han propuesto en la teoría psicológica reciente. Ella presenta las recomendaciones de una examinación de estos conceptos del yo en las entrevistas que ella dirigió en Guatemala con 40 adolescentes masculinos indígenas y latinos. Se discuten las implicaciones de esta investigación para los trabajadores de salud mental y se hacen sugerencias para el mejoramiento de servicios a esta población.

Introduction

A major shift in contemporary North American thinking about the nature of self arises from critiques of models that describe human nature as autonomous, independent, and individualistic and the moral ideal as principled, objective, rationally apprehended, and universal. Contemporary scholars are claiming that the self does not exist apart from relationships, that one is interconnected with others in essential ways, and that the moral ideal includes responsibility toward others, care, connection, and compassion. This redefinition of personhood and the moral ideal is clarified and examined through interviews with Guatemalan male youth about their values, their definitions of self, and their response to exposure to violence in Guatemala during the period from 1978 to 1982, a time of enormous internal disruption, violent civil strife, and family dislocation. The model of self revealed in these interviews is suggested as a source of psychological resilience that counselors working with displaced Guatemalan youth should recognize and acknowledge.

Theoretical Background: Conceptions of Self

The proclivity of contemporary Western culture to embrace individual autonomy and personal freedom has led us to advocate, out of Hobbesian concerns, that human rights be protected, civil rights be assured, and equal rights be attained. Recently, we have come to see, however, the limits of a moral view based entirely on concerns about individual rights and one that ignores responsibility to and inclusion of others (Bellah, Madsen, Sullivan, Swidler, A. & Tipton, 1985; Sandel, 1984). In 1971, feminist, sociologist, and critical observer of contemporary American culture, Elizabeth Janeway, presaged the critique of the autonomous, separate individual. Comparing the decade of the 1960s to that of the 1970s, Janeway wrote, "Where we once boasted that we are free, we are now more inclined to fear we are alienated." Robert Bellah and his colleagues sounded the alarm on the limits of American individualism, a trait observed by deTocqueville and found in interviews conducted during the 1970s across the United States. Within our achievement-oriented culture there is the nagging doubt that our stated concerns with individual rights and liberties may be in the service of more selfish aims than we have cared to admit and a dread that individualistic ambitions may have been achieved at the expense of community.

Reflections on and critiques of our contemporary cultural ethos can also be found in discussions about the nature of the person within the field of psychology. In 1977 Edward Sampson argued that American society needs an alternative to the individualistic, self-contained conception of person that is stifling our ability to solve social problems. More recently he boldly asserted: "Quite simply, understanding the individual qua individual is no longer relevant to understanding human life" (1989, p. 916). He stated that our view of persons as autonomous, separate individuals is a distortion because technological innovations make it possible to communicate with a wider world; our knowledge and informational boundaries cannot be contained as they once were; and our consciousness and even our rationality can no longer be assumed to be securely housed within our self-contained individuality. A case in point is the U.S. stock market plunge in October 1987 because of events occurring in Asian and European stock markets. Also, pollution is not bounded by geography, and the threat of nuclear annihilation is shared by the world community.

Sampson's message is familiar to feminist theorists and researchers, who have claimed that our cultural ethos is in need of change and is, indeed, changing (Brabeck, 1989). Feminism has been in the forefront in critiquing the dominant ideology. In the words of Jean Bethke Elshtain (1986), "To see feminism as an attempt to complete the promise of American democracy, or to make our social practices more consistent with our explicit political professions, is just part of the story. More important is the possibility that liberal principles alone cannot sustain liberal democracy; that, *in fact, our way of life ongoingly depends and has depended upon the survival of ties of community and obligation* unacknowledged, even suspect, within the dominant ideology" (p. 58, emphasis added). Furthermore, feminists are urging that our democratic systems must reflect the feminist ideals of connection and community if we are to survive the threat of nuclear annihilation and prevent the destruction of the earth's ecosystem (Ruddick, 1985). Feminists are arguing that a self defined in relationship with others, rather than a self defined as autonomous and individualistic, is better prepared to care for our fragile and explosive world. It is important to see this ideal of a self defined within relationship, a self developed through and inextricably tied to community, within its historical context.

Cross-cultural work supports the notion that there are different conceptions of self (Lykes, 1985, 1989; Sampson, 1988; Shweder & Bourne, 1982). Similar observations have been made by researchers studying subgroups in the United States. Luttrell's (1989) analysis of U.S. working class Black "women's ways of knowing" revealed distinctions in the sense of self and ways of making meaning that are affected by race and class as well as gender. Lykes's (1985, 1989) analysis of conceptions of self among "pink collar" workers and Guatemalan women living in exile in Mexico demonstrated the critical roles power, status, and material conditions exert on one's sense of self. Toinette Eugene (1989) described how material reality (one's economic, social, and power status, and one's cultural history) affects one's sense of self and gives rise to a feminist ethic of liberational care, found among Black women. Guatemalan youth show a similar conception of self that is tied to, and defined through, the community. Furthermore, their sense of self as part of a larger whole, a community, is an important factor in their resilience to the effects of exposure to the type of wide-scale violence that has characterized the experience of many in Guatemala, especially during recent decades. This violence has been especially devastating to the indigenous Mayans.

Background on Guatemala

Of the 8 million people in Guatemala, two thirds are pure-blood Indians (Indigenas), descendants of the ancient Mayans. Spanish is the official language of the country, but most Indigenas speak one of 22 totally separate languages (e.g., Cakchikel, Quiche, Mam, Tsutuil). The majority of the Mayan languages are spoken, not written, a factor that contributes to the illiteracy rate of over 60% in Guatemala and separates groups of Indigenas from each other. Even people living in villages nearby may not understand each other's language, a factor that may contribute to close community ties and may exacerbate the psychological consequences of forced relocation, even when the relocation site is within Guatemala.

Life expectancy is about 57 years among the Indigenas. This population has one of the highest infant mortality rates in the Western hemisphere (U.S. General Accounting Office, 1989b). Approximately 65% of the population lacks adequate health services, and the lack of potable water is a major cause of disease. According to UNICEF, 65% of Guatemalans have no access to health care, and the Economic Commission on Latin America reports that over 80% of all Guatemalan children under age 5 are malnourished (Guatemala Health Rights Support Project, 1989). It is tragic that the three leading causes of death in Guatemala—dehydration from diarrhea, respiratory illness, and violence—are all preventable. The uncertainty of life and the hardships of making a living contribute to the very close sense of community Guatemalans share and make even more poignant the hardships that have accompanied the civil war.

It is estimated that from 1980 to 1984, between 50,000 and 100,000 Guatemalans were killed, at least 38,000 of whom were victims of extrajudicial killings; many of these persons were forcibly taken from their homes, tortured, murdered, and left on the public highway to terrorize others into submission (Berryman, 1985; Carmack, 1988). Over 200,000 (and by some estimates as many as 500,000) Guatemalan children have lost one or both parents. In a country the size of Ohio, over 400 rural villages have been destroyed and over one million people, about one seventh of the population, have been displaced and forced to leave their homes and villages (Berryman).

A major cause of the war has been attributed to the unequal distribution of land in Guatemala (Lykes, 1989). About 66% of the arable land in Guatemala is held by 2.2% of the people (Lykes, 1989). The Mayans consider land sacred, as do the Native Americans of the United States. The Mayans value community over individualism and family ties are fundamental (Burgos-Debray, 1984), but their communities have been destroyed and their families displaced. In 1985, Archbishop Penados of Guatemala City stated that approximately one million people were internal refugees in their own country, forced to leave their villages, because the villages were destroyed or their lives threatened. Current estimates of persons still displaced in Guatemala, primarily throughout the highland area, are between 12,000 and 45,000 (U.S. General Accounting Office, 1989a). As of December 1988, approximately 41,200 Guatemalan refugees (UNHCR) and another 150,000 unregistered Guatemalans have sought refuge in Mexico (U.S. General Accounting Office, 1989a).

This research examines the indigenous values and sense of self found among an economically depressed but psychologically resilient and academically successful group of young men. The research on values and conceptions of self in interviews conducted in Guatemala during the summer of 1989 is part of a larger project being conducted in four countries (Guatemala, Argentina, Chile, and El Salvador) to examine the effects of war on children.

Subjects

Students in this study were attending a boarding school, which is equivalent to a U.S. high school plus 1 year of junior college. A total of 40 male students were interviewed in the summer of 1989; 9 were first-year students, 8 second-year, 10 third-year, 8 fourth-year, and 6 fifth-year. Ages ranged from 14 to 25; mean and mode were both 17. The range is relatively large because some boys missed school for as many as 3 years during the violent years. Admission to the school is very competitive; approximately 30% of applicants who apply finally matriculate. Acceptance is based on students' ability to speak Spanish, past academic record, intelligence test scores, values tests, profile of psychological health compiled by a Guatemalan psychologist, religious orientation and commitment, and ratings from interviews with at least three faculty members. Thus, the youths in this sample are intelligent, highly achieving, and in good physical and psychological health.

Approximately half ($n = 18$; 44%) of the boys interviewed came from what are called "conflicted areas" where, between 1978 and 1984, there was open conflict between the military and the guerillas as well as widespread disappearances and killings that affected primarily the Indigenas. These are also the areas where open conflict is found today (U.S. General Accounting Office, 1989b). The other ($n = 23$, 56%) students were from areas that were not as extensively involved in the conflict, though no area of Guatemala was immune from the terror. Seventeen percent ($n = 7$) of the students interviewed were Ladinos, mixed bloods, or persons who identified themselves as Ladinos. Eighty-three percent ($n = 34$) of the students were Mayan, for whom Spanish was a second language. Most had learned Spanish in school and spoke their native dialect at home. Students were chosen for the interview using the following criteria: Students who came from conflicted areas (which may account for the higher percentage of Indigenas in this study) were identified and selected; students who had passed the validity check of the Defining Issues Test (DIT), which was given to all students, and who were grade-equivalent with those in the previously selected group, also were accepted.

The young men in this study were economically disadvantaged. Most of their fathers worked as "campesinos," peasants on fincas farms who earned about 4 quetzales a day. At today's exchange rate (3.7 Q. to the dollar), the equivalent in U.S. money is about a dollar a day. One student's father made (sewed) shirts for 40 centavos (about 10 cents) a shirt. It costs approximately 500 U.S. dollars a year to educate each student (this includes laundry, food, maintenance of buildings, and salaries of staff and faculty). Each family is asked to pay something toward the tuition; many pay what is considered, by U.S. standards, a token fee—5 quetzales a month (U.S. $1.35).

Research Measures

The following measures were administered: (1) The Defining Issues Test (Rest, 1979: Spanish version translated by Carlos Canon from Bogota), a paper-and-pencil measure of moral reasoning; (2) an interview designed by Brinton Lykes to study the effects of war on children; (3) six Thematic Apperception Test pictures, modified by Lykes to be culturally relevant; (4) the Gilligan and Lyons (Lyons, 1983) questions to examine how the youth defined self, how they "defined themselves to themselves"; and (5) the Kinetic Family Drawing. The Defining Issues Test was administered in a separate group testing session that lasted 1 hour. The interviews were conducted in a small private office, were tape-recorded, and lasted between 1 and 1½ hours.

Results and Initial Observations

The students interviewed had all been exposed, directly or indirectly, to the violence in Guatemala. That is to say, as children between 1979 and 1984, many had seen tortured and murdered bodies that routinely were discarded on public roads; a number had friends or family members who had "disappeared" or were kidnapped and murdered; some had witnessed the murder of a parent, a brother, or an uncle. All had heard the stories of torture and disappearances. The boys in this study knew individuals and had family members who were widows and orphans. Ignacio Martin Baro (Martin-Baro, 1988) made the important point that state-sponsored violence affects all members within the state, whether or not they are victims of "direct" violence.

One of the boys in the study was working in the field with his father and other campesions, farmers, when the army came and rounded up a number of the men, his father among them, and took them away in a truck. The boy was 8 at the time. His father was later found, shot dead, his body left in a ravine. Another boy told the episode of the army coming to his village and assembling all the people in front of the church. They pointed to some of the men, lined them up against the wall, and shot them. What serves as a source of support and helps these youths handle the stresses that accompany exposure to such violence?

In comparison to Western samples, the students in this study scored low on the DIT. The overall average P (percent of principled reasoning) scores were 18.81. This average was computed on the tests that passed the validity checks described in the DIT scoring manual (Rest, 1979). The DIT scores obtained from this sample must be interpreted cautiously in light of the relatively large number ($n = 11$, 17%) that did not pass the validity checks. Language difficulties (Guatemalan boys took a test translated by a Colombian, and for many of the boys English was a second or even third language) and testing circumstances (the test was administered by a North American who is not fluent in the Spanish language) do not justify comparisons with other samples. These students will be retested in the near future to trace them longitudinally and to add a female sample.

Analysis of typed protocols of the interviews is in process. However, a preliminary observation from the interviews is relevant here. The Kinetic Family Drawing consists of instructions to "Draw everyone in your family, including yourself, doing something." It is followed by a series of questions. One of the questions was, "What are the desires, hopes of your family?" Initially students were asked, as per directions, to point to each member of the family and describe the individual's hopes and desires. The students, descendants of Mayan Indians, whose culture emphasizes community and connection among all living creatures (Burgos-Debray, 1984), pointed obediently to each person and repeated exactly the same hopes and desires for each person in the family. For example, one of the boys, call him Diego, pointed to his father and said, "He wants me to get a good education and help the family, and he wants us to be happy." He pointed to his brother and said, "He wants me to get a good education and help the family, and he wants us to be happy," and so it went with each member of the family. Diego was defining the collective desires of his family and attributing them to each individual. This happened so often that without making a conscious decision, the question was changed to, "What are the hopes and desires of your (collective) family?" The interview had been affected by the students' understanding of the connectedness of the individual members of the family.

This observation requires confirmation with more systematic analysis of the interviews, particularly the Gilligan and Lyons (Lyons, 1983) question, "How do you define yourself to yourself?" However, these young men were demonstrating Lykes's notion of "social individuality" and Sampson's notion of "ensembled individualism." These intelligent, socially adept, autonomously active students revealed a connection to their families in which their hopes and desires were not merely similar, but they were the same. These students derive their sense of self through the experience of community. They reflected the African adage that Sandra Crump, a colleague at Boston College, recently described: "We are, therefore, I am." This is a reversal of the Anglo-American philosophy that community arises in order to meet the needs of individuals. For the Mayan youth in Guatemala I interviewed, self may arise from and derive meaning through community. Furthermore, for these independent and achieving youths, the connections to family and community may serve an adaptive purpose. This would be consistent with recent findings (Kenny, 1989) that indicate that among U.S. adolescents, attachment, rather than separation, is associated with psychological adjustment. Counselors, steeped in North American cultural definitions of the mature self as independent and autonomous, may overlook the value of alternative models. In so doing, counselors may fail to acknowledge and reinforce an important source of psychological resilience.

References

Bellah, R., Madsen, R., Sullivan, W. M., Swidler, A., & Tipton, S. (1985). *Habits of the heart.* New York: Harper & Row.

Berryman, P. (1985). *Inside Central America.* New York: Pantheon.

Brabeck, M. (Ed.). (1989). *Who cares? Theory, research and educational implications of the ethic of care.* New York: Praeger.

Burgos-Debray, E. (Ed.). (1984). *I . . . Rigoberta Menchu: An Indian woman in Guatemala,* London: Verson.

Carmack, R. M. (Ed.). (1988). *Harvest of violence: The Maya Indians and the Guatemalan crisis.* Norman: University of Oklahoma Press.

Elshtain, J. B. (1986). *Meditations on modern political thought: Masculine/feminine themes from Luther to Arendt.* New York: Praeger.

Eugene, T. M. (1989). Sometimes I feel like a motherless child: The call and response for a liberational ethic of care by Black Feminists. In M. Brabeck (Ed.), *Who cares? Theory, research and educational implications of the ethic of care* (pp. 45–62). New York: Praeger.

Guatemala Health Rights Support Project. (1989). In hushed voices: Testimony of the Guatemalan Health Movement. 1747 Connecticut Ave., N.W., Washington, DC, 20009.

Janeway, E. (1971). *Man's world, woman's place.* New York: Morrow.

Kenny, M. (1989). College seniors' perceptions of parental attachment: The stability and value of family ties. *Journal of College Student Personnel, 38,* 17–29.

Luttrell, W. (1989). Working-class women's ways of knowing: Effects of gender, race and class. *Sociology of Education, 62,* 33–46.

Lykes, M. B. (1985). Gender and individualistic vs. collectivist bases for notions about the self. *Journal of Personality, 53.*

Lykes, M. B. (1989). The caring self: Social experiences of power and powerlessness. In Brabeck, M. *Who cares? Theory, research and educational implications of the ethic of care.* New York: Praeger.

Lyons, N. (1983). Two perspectives: On self, relationships and morality. *Harvard Educational Review, 53,* 125–145.

Martin-Baro, I. (1988). La violencia en Centroamerica: Una vision psicosocial. *Revista Costarricense de Psicologica, 12 & 13,* 21–34.

Rest, J. R. (1979). *Development in judging moral issues.* Minneapolis: University of Minnesota.

Ruddick, S. (1985). Maternal thinking and the practice of peace. *Journal of Education, 167*(3), 97–111.

Sampson, E. E. (1988). The debate on individualism: Indigenous psychologies of the individual and their role in personal and societal functioning. *American Psychologist, 43,* 15–22.

Sampson, E. E. (1989). The challenge of social change for psychology: Globalization and psychology's theory of the person. *American Psychologist, 44,* 914–921.

Sandel, M. J. (1984, May 7). Morality and the liberal ideal. *The New Republic,* pp. 15–17.

Shweder, R. A. & Bourne, E. J. (1982). Does the concept of the person vary cross-culturally? In A. J. Marsella & G. M. White (Eds.) *Cultural conceptions of mental health and therapy.* Boston: Reidel.

U.S. General Accounting Office. (1989a). *Central America: Conditions of Guatemalan refugees and displaced persons.* U.S. General Accounting Office. Report to Congressional Requesters, GAO/NSIAD-89-150, July.

U.S. General Accounting Office. (1989b). *Conditions creating refugees and U.S. asylum seekers from Central America.* Testimony of Thomas J. Schulz, Assistant Director, before the Commission for the Study of International Migration and Cooperative Economic Development, GAO/T-NSIAD-89-25, April.

Endnotes

1. Although the word "Indigena" (pronounced In-dee-he-nah) is translated frequently among English writers as "Indian," the Mayans prefer to translate it literally as "native" or "indigenous," and so I use it here.

2. On November 16, 1989, Ignacio Martin Baro, S.J., and five fellow Jesuits of the Central American University, along with their housekeeper and her 15-year-old daughter, were assassinated at Central American University. Ignacio Martin Baro was instrumental in designing the four-country study. Because of his death, and the escalation of the violence in El Salvador, it is uncertain how work in that country will proceed.

Career Development: A Comparative Cohort Study of Fifteen-Year-Olds in Mexico and the United States

Pedro A. Sanchez, Dorothy T. Soukup, and Silvia Pech Campos

Abstract

This paper aims to depict differences and similarities in the factors involved in career development for cohorts of 15-year-old students from Mexico and the United States. Responses on inventories measuring decision-making style, progress in choosing an occupation, locus of control, self-esteem, values involved in choosing an occupation, and educational expectations and sources of vocational information were collected from both samples. These data were compared by gender, nation, and socioeconomic status. Results suggest that two significant factors, nationality and gender, account for observed cultural differences in vocational behavior between the groups.

Resumen

Este artículo tiene la intención de representar las diferencias y las semejanzas de los factores que se envuelven en el desarrollo de carrera para los cohortes de estudiantes de quince años de México y de los Estados Unidos. Se recogieron de las dos muestras las respuestas en los inventarios que midieron el estilo de tomar una decisión, el progreso en seleccionar una carrera, el enfoque de control, la estima de sí, los valores envueltos en seleccionar una ocupación y las esperanzas educacionales y las fuentes de información vocacional. Se compararon estos datos según el género, la nación y el estado socioeconómico. Los resultados sugieren que dos factores significantes, el género y la nacionalidad, expliquen las diferencias culturales observadas en el comportamiento vocacional entre los grupos.

Introduction

Recognizing differences in cultural background has been highlighted as important to the vocational counselor when working with culturally different clients. Knowledge about the client's cultural milieu may help the counselor to understand better the origins, extent, and significance of cultural differences and is valuable in improving vocational counseling practices both in Mexico and in the United States. American counselors may gain insight into the culture-specific needs of Hispanic clients of Mexican origin, and Mexican counselors may better understand how to apply the knowledge of vocational psychology, as practiced in the United States, in their own practice.

It is assumed here that Mexican and U.S. societies provide qualitatively different environments in which adolescents grow up to be workers. Cross-cultural studies between Mexicans and North Americans have focused on general psychological differences. For example, Holtzman, Diaz-Guerrero, and Schwartz (1975) found three major differences between Mexican and U.S. children. First, Mexican boys and girls were more cooperative in interpersonal relationships, whereas their U.S. counterparts were more competitive. Second, Mexicans were more fatalistic and pessimistic. Third, Mexicans were more family-centered whereas U.S. children were more individualistic. In general, comparative studies have characterized U.S. society as competitive and individualistic whereas Mexican society has been described as an "interdependent social structure" (Holloway, Gorman, Gorman, & Fuller, 1987; Holtzman, 1982). Hence, cohorts from these two different societies are expected to exhibit different cultural values and psychological characteristics.

Very few well-designed, cross-cultural studies have been conducted on career development. The best known is the Work Importance Study (WIS), conducted by Nevill and Super (1986). They developed this study to identify the values an individual seeks in various life roles and the importance of the work role as a means of value realization. Nevill and Super used The Values Scale to obtain data from 10 different countries in Europe, the United States, and Asia. However, none of the countries included in this study were representative of the national origin of minority groups in the United States. For example, the majority of the Hispanic population in the United States is composed of individuals from Mexican, Cuban, and Puerto Rican origin. Yet, no cross-cultural studies have been conducted comparing North Americans and people from these countries. Therefore, our understanding of the career development of these minority groups is limited. The purpose of this study was to compare Mexican and U.S. adolescents on a number of psychological and sociocultural issues and the effect of these on career development.

Method

In cross-cultural research, it is important methodologically to recognize both the differences between groups as well as those within groups. Ponterotto (1988), in his comprehensive review of multicultural studies, stated: "[In] comparing one ethnic group with another, on some counseling variables the respective groups are perceived as homogeneous and . . . the tremendous heterogeneity existing within ethnic groups is ignored" (p. 414). In this study, age, location of school, religion, and gender were controlled in an attempt to make the groups homogeneous. Nonetheless, attention was paid to variability within the groups.

Subjects

A study of 298 students born in 1974 was conducted in the states of Iowa, U.S.A., and Yucatan, Mexico. Students from both countries were selected from urban, suburban, and rural schools. Mexican students were selected from the public school system. Because 98.5% of the Mexican population is Catholic, U.S. students were selected from private Catholic schools to homogenize both cohorts with regard to religion. Similarly, ethnic variability in the U.S. sample was minimal. Ninety-eight percent of the U.S. students were Caucasian.

Materials

The battery of instruments administered to the participants included a demographic questionnaire, a values scale, a checklist of appliances (to obtain an estimate of SES) and vocational information resources, and Harren's Assessment of Career Decision Making (Harren, 1976).

Procedures

Schools were chosen to be representative of three settings: rural (population less than 5,000), suburban (population between 10,000 and 20,000), and urban (population more than 50,000). Students were selected at random in the schools from lists of students born in 1974. Testing was conducted in a large group setting and took approximately 25 minutes. Tests were hand-scored by the researchers both in Mexico and the United States. Data were analyzed using PC Stats.

Results

Expectations

Overall, the U.S. sample showed significantly higher expectations for finishing high school and college as well as finding a satisfying future occupation. Particularly interesting is that women of both cultures (US $M = 89.7$; Mexico $M = 73.02$) were found to have higher expectations than men (US $M = 86.13$; Mexico $M = 64.78$) t (298) = 2.69, $P < .006$.

Socioeconomic Status (SES)

The distribution of the students' perception of socioeconomic status differed significantly in the samples. On a 4-point scale ranging from working class (1) to upper class (4), Mexicans were more evenly distributed across levels whereas U.S. students clustered in the upper middle-class level. Seventy-four percent of U.S. students considered themselves as upper middle class, but only 26% of the Mexicans considered themselves as upper middle class. Nine percent of the U.S. sample and 5% of the Mexican sample considered themselves as working class.

Vocational Values

In a hierarchy of 10 values important in choosing an occupation, both U.S. and Mexican students identified the same three values as most important: first, their liking of the occupation, second, future income, and third, their ability to perform the occupation. However, whereas the U.S. students clearly identified those three as being of paramount importance as compared with other values, the Mexicans' rank ordering of these values was more evenly distributed. The item "adequate to my gender" ranked ninth in the U.S. sample and fourth in the Mexican sample. In contrast, the item "reputation of the occupation" ranked fourth for the U.S. and tenth for the Mexican sample.

Vocational Information Resources

From a list of possible sources of vocational advice (e.g., parents, counselors, friends), the U.S. sample reported counselors (76%) and parents (70%) as the two sources most frequently consulted. Mexicans reported that parents (83%) were frequently consulted, and they also considered teachers (53%), siblings (51%), and counselors (41%) as important sources of advice.

Decision-Making Styles

Nationality was the major factor affecting decision-making styles. Both Mexican boys and girls were more rational than their U.S. counterparts. Neither nationality nor gender differences were found in intuitive styles. A randomized ANOVA with weighted means demonstrated significant differences between the countries in regard to the independence/dependence style $F(3, 286) = 6.69, P<.001$. A post-hoc Neuman-Keuls test showed that the differences between Mexican and U.S. boys accounted for the greatest amount of variance. In addition, U.S. girls were more independent than their Mexican counterparts $t(148) = 1.97, P<.05$.

Discussion

Important socioeconomic differences can be observed between the samples. Whereas most U.S. students were clustered in the upper middle-class status, the variability on the socioeconomic status was greater for Mexican students. Overall, the economic gap between the populations was marked.

Gender differences were apparent. Gender is an important issue in vocational decision making for Mexicans, but U.S. students give little importance to this factor. This can be explained by the more traditional roles Mexican women adopt as compared to their U.S. counterparts.

The role of the family, as an important support system within Mexican society, is illustrated by the influence that family members have on a student's vocational behavior. Whereas school counselors are often consulted on vocational issues in the United States, their role is secondary to that of family and teachers in Mexico. It is worth noting that there are very few counselors working in Mexican schools. Hence, teachers often assume the role of counselors in providing vocational advice. Although students in both samples were Catholic, only one student reported priests as a source of vocational advice. The fact that student-reported expectations were significantly lower for Mexican than for

U.S. students supports previous research findings characterizing Mexican society as pessimistic and fatalistic.

Several important counseling implications can be drawn from the findings of this study. First, counselors should be aware that whereas gender is a less important factor for U.S. students, it is of great importance in the vocational decision-making process for Mexicans. Second, counselors should be aware that many Mexicans have lower expectations about school achievement and occupational satisfaction. Because the relationship between high expectations and high school achievement has been well documented in the literature, counselors should especially encourage and motivate Mexican students. Third, counselors should be sensitive to the role and importance of the family in the vocational decision-making process of Mexican students. This is in contrast to the U.S. counselors' tendency to emphasize individualism and independence. Finally, differences in decision-making styles highlight the effects of cultural milieu over gender in determining cognitive aspects of vocational decision making. For example, whereas no differences were found between boys and girls in either of the three dimensions, Mexicans were more rational and dependent than their U.S. counterparts. Interestingly, the largest difference was found between boys. Mexican boys are significantly more dependent than U.S. boys. This finding supports the value of independence in U.S. society and shows that dependent decision-making practices are more congruent with cooperation within groups as portrayed by the Mexican sample.

References

Harren, V. A. (1976). *Assessment of Career Decision Making: Progress report.* Iowa City, IA: American College Testing Program.

Holloway, S. D., Gorman, L., Gorman, K., & Fuller, B. (1987). Child-rearing attributions and efficacy among Mexican mothers and teachers. *Journal of Social Psychology, 127*(5), 499–510.

Holtzman, W. (1982). Cross-cultural comparisons of personality development in Mexico and the U.S.. In D. Wagner & H. W. Stevenson (Eds.), *Cultural perspectives on child development.* San Francisco, CA: Freeman.

Holtzman, W. H., Diaz-Guerrero, R., & Schwartz, J. D., (1975). *Personality development in two cultures: Cross-cultural and longitudinal study of school children in Mexico and the United States.* Austin, TX: University of Texas Press.

Nevill, D., & Super, D. E. (1986). *The Values Scale Manual.* (Research edition). Palo Alto, CA: Consulting Psychologist Press.

Ponterotto, J. G. (1988). Racial/ethnic minority research in the Journal of Counseling Psychology: A content analysis and methodological critique. *Journal of Counseling Psychology, 35*(4), 410–418.

PART II

DIVERSITY

Many demographic and population changes are occurring throughout the Americas. In Central and South America there is increasing migration from rural to urban centers. In the United States, the Latino/Hispanic population has become the fastest growing minority group. Over 21 million persons of Latino/Hispanic origin now reside in the United States, and this number is expected to increase rapidly during the next century. Such demographic changes are affecting communities and social institutions in unprecedented ways. The language, educational, mental health, and other needs of these populations present important challenges to the counseling and human development profession. In order to meet these challenges, however, it is essential to understand the rich diversity within Latino/Hispanic groups. Furthering such an understanding is the purpose of the papers included in part 2 of this monograph.

The plenary paper by Richard Valencia and Martha Menchaca calls attention to the tremendous growth in the U.S. Latino/Hispanic population and the resulting implications. A historical overview of the immigration patterns of the Mexican-origin populations and their rich within-group diversity also is presented. Following the plenary paper, Veronica Kaune-Wilde reviews the literature with regard to establishing mental health center services for Latin Americans and makes recommendations for establishing such centers. Finally, Jairo Fuertes, William Sedlacek, and Franklin Westbrook discuss the findings of their research on Hispanic students attending a predominantly White university in the northeastern United States.

PLENARY ADDRESS

DEMOGRAPHIC OVERVIEW OF LATINO AND MEXICAN-ORIGIN POPULATIONS IN THE UNITED STATES: COUNSELING IMPLICATIONS

Richard R. Valencia and Martha Menchaca

Abstract

This session provides a demographic overview of the Latino/Hispanic population and a qualitative analysis of cultural diversity within the Mexican-origin population in the United States. Several questions regarding the socioeconomic status of Latino/Hispanics and implications for counseling and human development professionals are addressed. In addition, the historical roots of the Mexican-origin population and some of the special stressors they face are discussed. The authors conclude that counselor effectiveness can be enhanced through an understanding of cultural diversity within the Latino/Hispanic population.

Resumen

Esta sesión estipula una sobrevista demográfica de la población latinohispánica y un análisis cualitativo de la diversidad cultural dentro de la población de origen mexicano en los Estados Unidos. Se dirigen a muchas preguntas tocante a la condición socioeconómica de los latinohispánicos y las implicaciones para los profesionales consejeros y de desarrollo humano. En adición, se discuten las raíces históricas de la población de origen mexicano y algunos de los estreses especiales con los cuales se encaran. Los autores concluyen que la eficacia consejera puede mejorarse por una comprensión de la diversidad cultural dentro de la población latinohispánica.

Dr. Richard R. Valencia

This plenary address is to be considered as one unified presentation, although it is divided into two parts for the sake of discussion. My section is largely devoted to a descriptive, somewhat quantitative, demographic overview of Latino/Hispanic diversity. Dr. Martha Menchaca will present a qualitative analysis of cultural diversity within the Mexican-origin population in the United States of America.

Diversity is quite prevalent within Latin American countries. Mexico, for example, is a place where Spanish and dozens of Indian languages flourish. The Latino population in Latin America is also extremely large. Of the total population of 702 million people in the Americas, approximately 450 million people live in Latin America. That is a solid majority; 64% of the people from the southernmost tip of Chile to the North Pole, broadly viewed, are of Latino origin.

The large number of Latin American nationals in Central and South America and the Caribbean, as well as the various Latino/Hispanic groups in the United States, is indicative of the great degree of cultural diversity of Latino people. Approximately two of every three persons in the Americas are of Latin American background. Their presence is projected to increase substantially in the years ahead. With respect to the percentage of people living in Latin America and the Latino/Hispanics in the United States, demographers project that they will compose 72% of the population of the Americas in the year 2020. In other words, the non-Latino-origin population of the Americas was 36% in 1988; by the year 2020, the non-Latino population will be only 28%.

An analysis of current and projected future demographic patterns informs us of the immense cultural diversity and dramatic growth of the Latin American people. Those who live in the United States need to be aware of the growing presence of Latinos in their country as well as in Latin America in general. Perhaps one particular place to begin such an awareness is the United States, where there exists a chauvinistic claim to the exclusive ownership of the term "America." The United States must come to grips with the reality that America is a continent, not a country.

Let's now examine Latino/Hispanic diversity in the United States. In 1980 the national Latino population was nearly 15 million and accounted for about 7% of the total U.S. population of 228 million people. During the 1980s Latinos increased by nearly 6 million in the United States, and by the end of the decade they numbered 20.1 million. From 1980 to late 1989, the total U.S. population increased by only 9%. In contrast, the Latino population increased by a huge 40%, going from about 14 million to over 20 million. (Note: recent 1990 census data report 22.4 million Latinos.) The largest Latino group in terms of size is the Mexican-origin group, that is Mexican Americans or Chicanos, who compose approximately 63% of the total group. In descending order, they are followed by Central and South American people, Puerto Ricans, and Cubans.

With respect to where Latinos are located in the United States, we can conclude that they are not restricted to a particular location but are spread all over. Those of you who are here from California may realize that you come from a state in which about one third of all Latino people in the United States now reside, approximately 7 million. Texas is second, with about one in five of the population being Latino. New York follows with approximately 2 million Latinos, mostly Puerto Ricans. Florida has about 2 million Latinos, mostly Cubans. About 2 million Latinos (mostly of Mexican origin) live in Arizona, Colorado, and New Mexico. New Jersey is the home of approximately three fourths of a million Latino residents. The remaining states contain about 12% of the total Latino population. Regarding future growth projections, there are clear indications that the U.S. Latino population will continue to soar in the 1990s and well into the next century. Demographic trends indicate that by the year 2060, the

Latino population will number 54.2 million and will account for approximately one in five people of the total U.S. population of 310 million.

With regard to youth, using the year 1982 as the base and the population of newborns to age 17 as the target group, it is expected that the total U.S. youth population will increase by approximately 17% by the year 2020. That is, it will go from about 63 million in 1982 to approximately 73 million in the year 2020. Demographers note that the overall increase in the numbers of youths from now to 2020 will be driven by two major forces. First, the number of White youngsters during this 30-year period is actually expected to decline by 6 million, a 13% decline. On the other hand, the number of Chicano, Puerto Rican, and other Latino youths will more than triple, increasing from 6 million in 1982 to 19 million by the year 2020. They will make up one quarter of the total U.S. youth population. In short, the anticipated increase in the Latino youth population of nearly 13 million more than offsets the projected decline of 6 million in the White youth population. In fact, this remarkable increase in the Chicano and other Latino youth population will account for most of the overall growth in the youth population expected between 1982 and the year 2020. In summary, in the decades ahead, our nation will witness a profound transformation of its youth population. Almost 3 in 4 children in 1982 were White; by 2020 only about 1 in 2 will be White. In 1982 only 1 in 10 children was Latino. By 2020, about 1 in 4 is projected to be Latino.

It is important to pause and ask ourselves: In light of the tremendous growth and accompanying diversity in the U.S. Latino population, how likely are Latinos to fare in the quest for a better life? Concurrent with their booming population, will Latinos also gain political power? Will they attain socioeconomic mobility? Will they obtain better schooling? Will they attain a sense of personal contentment and fulfillment?

In recent years, there has been some optimism that many aspects of life for U.S. Latinos will improve. For example, accompanying the national attention that Chicanos and other Latinos received in the late 1970s and early 1980s was the often-stated claim that the 1980s would be the "decade of the Hispanic." There were expectations within and outside the larger Latino community that Chicanos, Puerto Ricans, and other Latinos would benefit from their growing presence. Gains were anticipated along educational, economic, political, and general quality-of-life aspects. However, contrary to the expected gains during the decade of the Hispanic, the 1980s left many Latinos, particularly Chicanos and Puerto Ricans, worse off. The National Council of La Raza, which is an advocacy organization for Latinos based in Washington, DC, recently produced an important report called "The Decade of the Hispanic: A Sobering Economic Retrospective." Seven trends that characterized Latinos' economic condition during the 1980s were identified:

1. Latinos benefitted least from the economic recovery of the 1980s in that their income stagnated and high rates of poverty continued. For example, in 1979, 22% of Latinos in the United States were poor. In 1988 the rate jumped to nearly 30%.
2. Latinos had a higher rate of children living in poverty in 1988 than they did in 1979.
3. There were no economic improvements for Latino households.
4. Latino married couples and families experienced deepened hardships; poverty rates increased.
5. There was widening income disparity. For example, Latinos in 1988 were 14% more likely to make under $10,000 a year than they were in 1979.

6. Although some areas showed slight educational gains, Latinos overall continued to feel the full impact of the educational crisis. For example, in 1978, 13% of Latino families with householders who actually had completed 4 years of high school lived in poverty. In 1988 the figure climbed to 16%. In addition, Chicano students now have the dubious distinction of being the most undereducated of our nation's large ethnic minority groups.

7. Although Latino 12-month, full-time workers showed a very slight increase in earnings from 1979 to 1988, male Latino workers' earnings during this period dropped approximately by an average of $3,000 a year.

In summary, one can conclude that things do not look very good for Latinos in the United States. As people who have experienced long-standing oppression, it is likely that Latinos will continue to face a host of institutional and personal stressors that thwart their progress. This contention is based, of course, on the presumption that the status quo will go unchallenged. We believe that specialists in the counseling and human development field should join Latinos in the struggle for equality and a better life. These professionals can be advocates and shapers of multiculturalism, bilingualism, and personal and political empowerment.

Counselors and other human development specialists, through their one-on-one work, are in an excellent position to learn from Latinos as well as to provide them with insight and guidance in realizing their goals. How might you and others actually engage in these learning and helping activities with Latinos? Well, that is a major topic of this conference. My perusal of the topics of the numerous workshops and papers of the conference inform me that you have many ideas to share and discuss regarding counseling and human development services for Latinos. In any event, the task before Dr. Menchaca and me is to introduce and address the theme of diversity. Thus far I have introduced, very broadly, Latino diversity. But in order for human development specialists to clarify their roles as professionals and advocates for Latino people, it is necessary that they attain a closer sense of the cultural diversity among Latinos. This analysis is an enormous undertaking; therefore, in the interest of time and what is humanly possible here, we have confined ourselves to a sliver of the Latino experience. Dr. Martha Menchaca will now focus on diversity within the Mexican-origin, that is, the Chicano population in the United States. We have selected Chicanos as our reference group for two reasons. First, the Chicano people account for about 6 of every 10 Latinos in the United States. Thus, by their mere numbers, they demand attention. Second, based on our own personal histories and our scholarly work, we are most familiar with the Chicano people and their experience. Dr. Menchaca will now analyze diversity within the Mexican-origin population in the United States.

Dr. Martha Menchaca

Dr. Valencia has provided a general overview of the Latino population in the United States. I will focus on one Latino group, the U.S. Mexican-origin population. This presentation will explore cultural issues related to diversity, which should be of use to those counseling and human development specialists who have Mexican-origin clientele or who are concerned about this population.

Anthropological studies indicate that the Mexican-origin population's main source of cultural diversity stems from their generational residence in the United States. Period of migration has strongly conditioned their cultural formation. This issue will become clear in the presentation as I move forward. Before I discuss variance within the Mexican-origin population, I will briefly review their migration history. This will provide a contextual background to understand this ethnic group's cultural characteristics.

All Chicanos are erroneously stereotyped as a newcomer immigrant group in the United States. Allegedly, they arrived after the Northern European migrants. Mexican settlements in the United States actually began as early as 1598, when Hispano settlers established colonies in northern New Mexico. The first colonies were established by mestizos (people of Spanish-Indian ancestry), who intermarried and battled the American Indians. Throughout the 17th and 18th centuries, Mexican settlements were established. In Arizona settlements were established in 1680, in Texas in 1716, and in California in 1769. The era of Mexican migration expanded in the late 1800s, when thousands of Mexicans entered the United States in an attempt to escape the repressive Mexican "hacienda" system. During this period, families who resided along the border of northern Mexico also resettled in the U.S. border region. These families, unlike the hacienda migrants, decided to settle in the United States in order reunite their extended kin. Many of the families had been separated by the political aftermath of the Mexican-American War of 1846 to 1848, and as a consequence the families reunited in the American Southwest, rather than in northern Mexico.

Another major period of Mexican migration occurred between 1910 and 1927. This migration was stimulated by economic and political forces. Mexicans were being driven out by the Mexican revolution and the civil unrest that followed. Concurrently, they were being attracted to the United States by the availability of employment, particularly within the California agricultural industry. Mexican migration once again peaked during World War II. This time, however, it was closely administered and controlled by the U.S. government. In 1942, the United States and Mexico enacted a binational guest workers program for Mexicans. Mexican men were extended a 6-month contract to work in American farms. The program was eventually called the Bracero Program.

The Bracero Program had a large impact on the U.S. Mexican community in that it contributed to the dramatic growth of the Mexican immigrant and undocumented populations. Thousands of Mexican immigrants settled in the United States during this period, and thousands of undocumented workers crossed the border in search of work. Researchers estimate that between 1942 and 1964 approximately 5 million immigrants settled in the United States, and 5 million Mexicans entered clandestinely.

During the mid-1960s the legal status of most Mexican newcomers was destined to be undocumented. In 1965 the U.S. government reformed its immigration and naturalization laws, making most of the Mexican working class ineligible to apply for immigration. This legislation commenced the era of the undocumented. During the 1970s to 1990s, Mexicans continued to migrate to the United States in large numbers despite their inability to be documented. This was particularly true during the early to mid-1980s, when Mexico experienced a new economic crisis related to the oil industry. However, many of the undocumented who entered the United States during this period will be receiving amnesty as a result of the Immigration Reform and Control Act (IRCA) of 1986. We do not know what the consequences of IRCA will be. If this population is legalized, social scientists will then be able to study them and learn about how they differ or are similar to the rest of the Mexican-origin people residing in the United States.

I will now move on and describe the type of diversity within the Mexican-origin population. The diverse ethnic labels Mexican-origin people use will be a starting point. Mexican-origin people in the United States call themselves by various ethnic labels such as Chicano, Mexican American, Mexican, Mexicano, Hispano, Hispanic, and Latino. Variance in labels is motivated by generational, regional, and political differences. For example, many whose ancestors date back before the U.S. conquest of the Mexican North seem to prefer the term Spanish, such as the northern New Mexican Hispanos who settled in the Southwest during the 16th and 17th centuries. These people recognize that they are part of the Mexican-origin people of the United States. However, because their ancestors migrated to the Southwest during the Spanish period (1958 to 1821), they identify as a Hispano Southwestern ethnic group rather than as Mexican. This group identifies more closely with their American Indian and Spanish ancestry.

A second group of people who do not label themselves as Mexicans are the Mexican Americans who became part of the middle class in the 1920s, as well as many of the GI families of the 1940s. Their identity, however, was formed by different social forces in comparison to the northern New Mexican Hispanos. Scholars have found that pressures brought by outside oppression forced many, particularly in earlier decades, to hide their Mexican origin under the euphemisms "Spanish" or "Latin American." These individuals led their children to call themselves Americans or Latins in an effort to disassociate themselves from Mexico and its economic problems. Surveys indicate, however, that since the 1960s this group has shifted back to using ethnic labels stressing their Mexican ancestry. Overall, the current use of the terms Mexican, Mexican American, Mexicano, and Chicano indicates that there is a strong sense of pride in identifying with Mexican culture.

Acculturation is another area of diversity. Different levels of Anglo-American acculturation are manifested within the Mexican-origin population. It is inaccurate to assume, however, that the longer a person has lived in the United States the more Anglicized he or she becomes and the less Mexican. A common misconception is that the culture of Mexican-origin people can be measured by using a unilateral compendium where at one end of the scale are the Mexican immigrants and on the other the U.S.-born, urbanized Chicanos.

The stereotype is that a Mexican immigrant is agrarian in dress style, a farm laborer, and poor. In contrast, the U.S.-born Chicano leads an urban lifestyle, no longer works in farm labor, and is middle-class. A second misunderstanding about cultural change is the perspective that the Mexican-origin population will move up the mobility ladder just as the European ethnic groups did, and that their economic advancement will surely proceed into the mainstream at all assimilation levels. This perspective downplays the role of racial prejudice in the United States and stresses that if Mexicans disassociate themselves from their cultural ancestry, they will become socially and economically integrated.

Human beings are not controlled by a continuum that gives them no choice and, as Dr. Valencia pointed out, generational residence produces cultural change but it does not ensure upward mobility. Chicanos do not automatically become wealthy when they shed their Mexican ancestry. Abundant evidence indicates that Chicanos are pressured to change their culture to conform to Anglo norms, but are not rewarded economically for doing so. Acculturation for the Mexican-origin population must be viewed as a larger process of ethnic retention and cultural loss. Some traditions and ideas have been maintained, such as the Mexican kinship structure. Others, such as the agrarian dress style, have been shed. Sometimes traditions are mixed with old and new practices. Southwestern food, which is based on Mexican-American Indian recipes using U.S. products, is an example of how practices are combined.

Generational residence in the United States does produce cultural change in the areas of family, language, legal status, and marriage patterns. Regarding language, for example, there is a pattern among the children of immigrants to shift from being dominant Spanish speakers to becoming either bilingual, or monolingual English speakers. We cannot assume, however, that Mexican-origin people lose their ability to communicate in Spanish by the second or third generation. Their fluency does decrease, but it is interesting to note that they exhibit a great deal of Spanish language loyalty. Based on 1980 census data, the Spanish language seems to be of great significance to them. The data indicated that from 14 million Spanish-surnamed people in the United States, only 21% lived in families that spoke only English and 79% lived in bilingual or Spanish monolingual households, where one or more than one family member spoke Spanish.

Another issue of diversity is the Mexican kinship structure. The traditional view of the Mexican-origin family postulates that with longer generational residence in the United States, the extended Mexican kinship structure will be shed and replaced by the Anglo-American nuclear family structure. This perspective depicts the Mexican kinship structure to be characterized by a large extended family that resides in the same household. Scholars have found that this perspective may have existed in the agricultural camps of the early 1900s, but today it is a misconception. For example, research indicates that although Mexican-origin people place a great emphasis on developing emotional support networks among the extended family, this does not mean that all cousins, aunts, and uncles reside in the same household or that they share each other's income. The extended family is an emotional support network. Individuals select certain relatives to be part of their family network while excluding other relatives. The extended family is not a parasitic economic structure where the upwardly mobile have to support financially the relatives who are economically unstable.

The role of patriarchy within the family is of course an issue of diversity. It is unfortunate, however, that in the United States many people assume that all Mexican-origin families practice the same type of gender relations. Research indicates that a gender structure characterized by patriarchal dominance is a worldwide cross-cultural phenomenon. Moreover, within all cultures there are group variances. Some families adopt patriarchal practices and ideas whereas other families practice more egalitarian traditions. The same type of group variance applies to Mexican-origin families. For example, a study conducted at Stanford University (Segura, 1987) examined how the family affected the achievement level of the Chicanas. In this study 200 Chicana PhDs, MDs, and JDs were surveyed to explore which factors encouraged them to pursue a higher education. All the Chicanas reported that their families were their main source of emotional support, encouraging them to complete higher education. What does this study tell us? Can we conclude that all Chicanos encourage the women in the family to pursue a higher education? Of course not; however, it does point to diversity within Mexican-origin families.

Another issue of diversity is the size of the Mexican kinship structure. Anthropological studies indicate that the Mexican kinship structure does not disappear with increasing generations in the United States. On the contrary, the size of the extended family increases with succeeding generations in the United States. Mexican immigrants have the smallest family size, and second and third generation Chicanos have the largest extended families. The latter two groups maintain large extended family networks and intimate relations with their favorite relatives. This pattern occurs in both urban and rural areas.

On the other hand, anthropologists have also found that immigration strongly influences the Mexican kinship structure. As a result of several factors, many Mexican families gradually terminate their relations with their relatives in Mexico. For example, the distance between the United States and Mexico and the existence of a border lessen interaction and create social distance between relatives. The children of the newcomers, having few relatives in the United States, resume the extended family structure upon marriage with U.S. residents.

Another important area of diversity is found in interethnic marriage patterns. Data on intermarriage indicate that the majority of marriages among Mexican-origin people continue to be within their ethnic group. A significant number of studies indicate, however, that interethnic marriages are on the rise. Several studies cited by Feagin (1990) found that in Texas and New Mexico outside-the-group marriage patterns range from 5% to 25%, and in California from 34% to 36%. Some of the studies in California, however, have been criticized for having very small sample sizes and not being representative of the population. (Interestingly, several studies have also shown that Chicanos who marry outside their group often select Latin American spouses.)

Mexican-origin people are also distinguished by their place of birth and legal status. Place of birth differentiates the U.S.-born from Mexican nationals. Studies indicate that Mexican nationals maintain closer ties to Mexico, listen more often to Spanish language stations and music, and have more family members who are Spanish-speaking monolinguals. They also like to celebrate Mexican national holidays more often than do their U.S.-born counterparts. Furthermore, within the Mexican national population of the United States, legal status tends to generate differences between the documented and undocumented. However, because of the difficulty in collecting data about undocumented migrants, most current research focuses on topics related to the labor market. For example, studies indicate that within the agricultural industry, the better-paid and year-round positions are reserved for Mexican immigrants who are legal residents. The undocumented, in contrast, are hired primarily for seasonal employment and are paid lower wages. As a consequence, undocumented workers migrate throughout the United States in search of employment.

The topic of the undocumented brings us now to a very important issue that can help the counseling and human development professionals serve their Mexican-origin clientele. Understanding diversity among the Mexican-origin population is extremely important for these professionals in order to have a realistic view of these people instead of a simple, stereotyped perspective. Undocumented status, inability to speak English, racist stereotyping, and seasonal farm labor employment are some of the psychological stressors related to diversity that should be of concern to counseling and human development professionals. Undocumented immigrants experience psychological stress related to their fear of being detected, apprehended, and deported. Among adults, this fear is often based on the realization that if they are apprehended they will lose their jobs, possibly be separated from their family, and most likely will experience humiliation when their friends find out that they are not Mexican immigrants.

The inability to speak English is a second psychological stressor. Often, Spanish speakers experience feelings of inadequacy when they are unable to communicate with their employers, doctors, coworkers, teachers, and service providers. They also fear being manipulated and being taken advantage of. Their fears are not unwarranted. In a review of the literature on public services for Mexican-origin people, Feagin (1990) found that Mexicans are often not provided with interpreters in hospitals, clinics, and police departments. It is also common that in a courtroom a Mexican is defended by an attorney who has limited Spanish proficiency, and the case is heard by a judge who does not understand Spanish.

Racism is a third psychological stressor. Although by the 1960s and 1970s some of the stereotypes were beginning to fade from public view, many prejudicial attitudes continue. For example, drunkenness and criminality are often attributed to Chicanos. Movies often depict Chicanos as bandits or servants. It is also common for comedians on television to get laughs by falsely depicting Chicanos to be Cholos or what we call in Mexico, pachucos. They also stereotype them as being criminals, drug addicts, or simply buffoons who speak with a funny accent. Chicanos also continue to be discriminated against in the schools. Chicanos continue to be a highly segregated ethnic group, and in many cities Anglo-Americans are resistant to desegregating the schools. Chicanos are also often stereotyped as being intellectually inferior and dirty. In a survey conducted in a central California city, one quarter of the Anglo-American respondents stated that they would find it distasteful to eat with a Mexican, and 37% stated that Mexicans were shiftless and dirty. In my own university, one administrator was recently demoted for publicly stating that Mexican American college students were intellectually inferior and that they lowered university standards. In sum, racism, regardless of how it is manifested, angers most Mexican-origin people and is a major source of psychological stress.

Employment instability is also a well-known source of psychological stress. Farm workers who are unable to find year-round employment must migrate throughout the United States seeking seasonal farm jobs. Employment instability produces psychological stress for all age groups. For example, parents are concerned that the rancher will not pay them a fair wage. Moreover, they are concerned that when they migrate throughout the United States in search of work, crops may be destroyed by the weather. Parents and children are also stressed by the fact that when they have to move to the next job, the children will be pulled out of school. The children of farm workers are also concerned with the stigma attached to farm labor. Within many communities, farm labor continues to be one of the most undesirable occupations. It is not uncommon for intergenerational conflict to erupt between parents and children because of the family's occupation. The children of farm workers are often embarrassed that their parents are migrant agricultural workers.

In closing, counselors and human development specialists can better help Chicanos improve their quality of life by understanding that diversity exists within the Mexican-origin population. With such an understanding, professionals will be better prepared to provide services and therefore help these clients to solve their problems and realize their goals.

References

Feagin, J. (1990). *Racial and ethnic relations*. Englewood Cliffs, NJ: Prentice-Hall.
Segura, D. (1987). Labor market stratifications: The Chicana experience. In R. Takaki (Ed.), *From different shores: Perspectives on race and ethnicity in America*. Oxford and New York: Oxford Press.

Providing Culturally Sensitive Human Development Services for Latin Americans

Veronica Kaune-Wilde

Abstract

The author reviews the literature regarding what human service providers must know in order to provide culturally sensitive counseling and human development services for Latin Americans. Emphasis is placed on the details of conducting a needs assessment for establishing a counseling center serving this population. The importance of community involvement and support in implementing the needs assessment is stressed. The author concludes with specific guidelines for data gathering and human development service delivery.

Resumen

La autora repasa la literatura tocante a lo que los provisores de servicios humanos tienen que saber para proveer los consejos y los servicios de desarrollo humano de una manera culturalmente sensible a los latinoamericanos. Se pone énfasis en los detalles de dirigir una valoración de necesidades para establecer un centro de consejos que sirva esta población. Se subraya la importancia del enredo y del apoyo de la comunidad para realizar la valoración de necesidades. La autora concluye con directivas específicas para el recogimiento de datos y la entrega de servicio de desarrollo humano.

Introduction

To provide culturally sensitive counseling and human development services for Latin Americans, human service providers (HSP) need to pay attention to two issues: They should know how to assess Latin Americans' needs, and they must provide counseling services in a culturally appropriate manner. This paper discusses conclusions derived from the review of the literature about these issues.

Statement of the Problem

Gonzales (1976) and Alarcon (1986) pointed out the scarcity and inappropriate distribution of resources to confront the diversity of mental health problems in Latin

America. They argued that the observable difference in human development services in various regions of Latin America is related to their socioeconomic and sociopolitical development. In many areas of Latin America mental health services have been neglected. The authors stated that the social conditions of many developing countries contribute to mental health problems. Gonzales suggested that new technologies, unemployment and underemployment, family disorganization, unreachable goals, and unfulfilled aspirations contribute to mental health problems in developing countries.

Peroto (1975) addressed the need for human development centers in Bolivia. He emphasized that they could be a valuable asset for the general population. However, he pointed out that their establishment could be difficult due to the country's social and economic instability. There is a general scarcity of decentralized human development services in Latin America. Therefore a great need exists to educate the governments and the people about the importance of such services. It is also important to recognize that Latin American countries are pluralistic societies. Therefore, a cross-cultural modality should be considered when providing services to these populations. Otherwise, language, ethnic and racial factors, and class-bound and culture-bound values can act as barriers (Sue, 1981).

Assessing Latin Americans' Needs

Culturally sensitive counseling and human development services for Latin Americans start with a culturally specific needs assessment. HSP need to take into account Latin America's culture, subcultures, norms, and values (Humm-Delgado & Delgado, 1983). Community involvement is imperative to conduct a successful needs assessment study (Cohen, 1976; Flaming, 1976; Josephson, 1970; Ryan, 1980; Vasquez & Uhlig, 1978).

In order to do a culturally sensitive needs assessment, HSP need to define the population, select appropriate methodology, gain entry, obtain support and publicity from the community they attempt to assess, choose and train staff, and interpret, present, and use the findings (Humm-Delgado & Delgado, 1983). A Latino advisory committee should be formed to assist in the needs assessment. Interactive or impressionistic approaches, such as key informants, community forums, and community surveys work best with this population. On the other hand, noninteractive or hard approaches, such as social indicators, demographic analysis, or rates-under-treatment approaches, are not very useful when assessing Latin Americans' needs, principally because of a lack of accurate census data on the Latino population (Humm-Delgado & Delgado, 1983, 1986).

The first step in needs assessment, gaining entry into the Latino community, has to be considered seriously. HSP' entry into the community can be enhanced by interagency collaboration, by developing an effective Latin American advisory committee, by involving natural support systems throughout the needs assessment, by increasing their own awareness of informal health systems (e.g., folk healers), by understanding Latin American norms and values, and by taking advantage of local media and institutions (Humm-Delgado & Delgado, 1986; Hurst & Zambrana, 1980; Josephson, 1970; Vasquez & Uhlig, 1978).

Finally, needs assessment researchers must present findings of the study and disseminate the results bilingually to the community in a nontechnical manner. The community should feel empowered and recognize that their cooperation contributed to tangible efforts, such as the development of a new program, modification of existing programs, or presentation of a written report in English and Spanish. Failure to present the findings might discourage the community and limit future needs assessment endeavors (Humm-Delgado & Delgado, 1983; Rosado, 1980).

Counseling Latin Americans

Before attempting to counsel with Latin American populations, counselors must be aware of their culture, norms, and values. Counselors must be aware of and understand: (a) the Latin American family system (nuclear, extended, and co-parenting), which is a very strong source of support for the Latin American client (Abad, Ramos, & Boyce, 1974); (b) that gender roles are rather rigid and clearly defined, with the man as the authority figure and the woman the nurturing, loving person who attempts to meet family needs (Padilla, 1981); (c) the role of personalism, the preference for close personal contact between Latinos (Ruiz & Padilla, 1977); (d) that Latin Americans' time orientation is in the here-and-now (Rivera, 1978); and (e) that the Latin American concept of well-being refers to both psychological and physical aspects (Padilla, Ruiz, & Alvarez, 1975). Counselors must also consider (f) acculturation (the degree to which an individual is part of the majority cultural group) (Padilla, 1980; Ruiz & Padilla, 1977); (g) locus of control, with many Latin Americans tending to have an external locus of control because of poor environmental conditions (Ruiz & Padilla); (h) the importance of respect, which is present in all interactions, especially when dealing with older persons (Abad et al., 1974); (i) the role of confianza (trust) and mutual respect as a cultural glue for relationships among Latin Americans (Velez, 1980); (j) religion as a very important source of support for Latin Americans (Abad et al.); (k) the folk healer system, an important informal health system used by many, but not all, Latin Americans (Abad et al.); and (l) language and dialects (Spanish, Quechua, Aymara, Guarani, Portuguese, etc.). It should be noted that authors like Ruiz (1985), Acosta and Cristo (1981), and Marcos (1976) suggest that clients' emotional problems are better dealt with in their first language.

It is also important for counselors to take into account Latin Americans' attitudes toward mental health. It seems that many Latin Americans have a positive attitude toward mental health (LeVine & Padilla, 1980); however, some authors emphasize that inappropriate assessment of Latin American attitudes may account for their low utilization of services (Keefe, 1979; Sue, 1981). It is suggested that Latin Americans be educated about the purpose and mission of human service agencies through orientation programs. This approach has been applied successfully to increase clients' utilization of services (Acosta, Evans, Hurwicz, & Yamamoto, 1987; Normand, Inglesias, & Payn, 1974).

Counselors must also learn the meaning of the major folk illnesses in relation to the folk healer system. They include susto (fright), mal de ojo (evil eye), mal puesto (bad state), mal aire (bad air), empacho (constipation), and caida de mollera (fallen fontanella) (LeVine & Padilla, 1980).

It is also important to consider clients' socioeconomic and cultural conditions in order to select an appropriate therapeutic intervention. Clients may be in a state of stress because of external reasons such as poverty, lack of jobs, or malnutrition (LeVine & Padilla, 1980). Knowing a client's socioeconomic background will assist in selecting a directive or nondirective approach for counseling. There is controversy regarding which approach is more appropriate for Latin Americans. Some authors like Abad et al. (1974), Torrey (1972), Ruiz and Casas (1981), and Sue (1977) argue against non-directive approaches, saying they are "cheap talk" and do not help clients with problems such as poverty. These authors consider directive approaches more suitable in helping to recognize problems, make decisions, and find solutions. However, authors like Padilla (1981) state that middle-class Latin Americans might benefit from insight counseling. Overall, it seems that the appropriate approach is dictated by the individual's education, locus of control, and socioeconomic background. Individual differences must always be considered in deciding which approach will benefit the client (LeVine & Padilla, 1980).

The first interview with the client is crucial. It is important for counselors to determine if clients are knowledgeable about the counseling process; if not, clients must be educated about mental health and the purpose of the agency. During the interview, communication styles should be considered. Latin Americans tend to self-disclose little at the beginning of the counseling process; the counselor must determine if it is due to cultural aspects or resistance (Velasquez & Velasquez, 1980). These authors state that during the first interview, counselors might want to employ the bicultural continuum tool in assessing the client's degree of biculturalism, which can also help determine the course of counseling.

Some therapeutic modalities have been found to be effective when counseling Latin Americans. These are: (a) pluralistic counseling and therapy, (b) family therapy, (c) psychodrama, (d) cognitive-behavioral approaches, (e) assertiveness training, and (f) group counseling. Pluralistic counseling is considered particularly relevant because it can be used as a general framework to counsel Latin Americans. Pluralistic counseling is defined as a modality that recognizes a client's culturally based beliefs, values, behaviors, and adaptation to her or his particular milieu (LeVine & Padilla, 1980). This approach is sensitive to all facets of a client's personal and family history as well as social and cultural orientation, and it is vigilant to the ways culture affects the individual. Its goal is to help clients clarify their personal and cultural standards. The pluralistic counselor must be aware of cultural differences. The counselor assists clients to interpret their emotional problems in terms of the client's worldview, and points out system maladjustments according to the client's cultural conceptions.

Culturally sensitive counselors should be aware of their own lifestyles, biases, and stereotypes about their own culture and others' (Pine, 1972). They should also be aware of the impact of socioeconomic and sociopolitical forces on the minority client. Effective cross-cultural counselors have as a major goal the amelioration of personal distress caused by oppression. They enhance clients' self-concepts and appreciation of their cultural roots by fostering pride in their culture. In addition, counselors can act as effective change agents in reshaping institutions toward nonprejudicial actions as well as educating about changes in gender roles. Effective counselors should not avoid issues of prejudice and racism; they should help clients deal with and change such discriminatory practices.

It is also necessary that cross-cultural counselors educate the Latino population about the mission, purpose, and goals of counseling. This educational process can occur in schools, hospitals, churches, and social clubs (LeVine & Padilla, 1980; Sue, 1981). The literature is contradictory on whether or not it is beneficial that counselors counsel only clients from their own culture. Some studies show that a difference in a counselor's and a client's culture does not necessarily affect counseling. Research in this area is needed. It is the author's experience that as long as counselors are fully aware of and knowledgeable about the culture of those they attempt to help, ethnicity and race is not necessarily an issue.

In order to deliver culturally sensitive and appropriate human services to Latin Americans, human service agencies must be located in the community they attempt to serve and their staff must be bicultural and bilingual. The agency must involve natural support systems (extended family, folk healer, religious leaders). Integrative services such as education, career counseling, activities for the community, and training and help in administrative matters (Abad et al., 1974; Padilla, Ruiz, & Alvarez, 1975; Phillips, 1971; Tsung-Yi Lin, 1984) should be included.

Guidelines for Providing Services to Latin Americans

The following guidelines are offered for human services providers attempting to assess needs and provide human development counseling services to Latin Americans:

1. Before stating the purpose of the human development center, HSP must assess the needs of the population they plan to assist. A first step is to become well acquainted with the target population: to become aware of, learn about, and understand its culture, norms, values, traditions, attitudes, and behaviors.

2. HSP should learn who the community leaders are and gain their trust in order to gain entry into the community. By establishing trust between community leaders and HSP, a foundation is laid.

3. Researchers, counselors, community members, and institutions that represent the community should be integrated into an advisory committee.

4. The advisory committee can conceptualize, discuss, and implement issues; determine the goals, mission, and purpose of the needs assessment; determine the appropriate approaches to be used; and assist in networking with key persons within the community. Community involvement at these early stages of the needs assessment project enhances rapport and develops a community's sense of ownership of the project.

5. Interactive approaches such as a community survey, key informant, and community forum are useful when assessing Latin American needs.

6. To ensure community involvement, community members can be trained as interviewers to work with HSP.

7. Once data have been gathered, results should be analyzed within the community's cultural context with the assistance of the advisory committee. Findings should be presented to the community to elicit feedback. HSP should interpret data accurately and not impose their biases. By presenting the results, the HSP show they are reliable, responsible, dependable, and trustworthy.

8. Once needs have been determined, the HSP in conjunction with the community can determine the kind of human development center that will be most helpful and choose an appropriate name for it.

9. The center should take into account the community's culture, traditions, and norms. It should provide services in a holistic, integrative manner; these should include counseling and psychotherapy, career counseling, education, advocacy, employment, health services activities for the community, training paraprofessionals, and helping individuals with administrative matters. The center should be located within the community and should reflect the community's culture through Latin American paintings, colors, and music, among other manifestations.

10. The center should provide direct walk-in and by-appointment services with bilingual and bicultural staff. Ideally the staff should be made up of counselors, psychologists, physicians, educators, folk healers, and other trained paraprofessionals. Policies with regard to seeing clients should be flexible, entailing not using the standard 50-minute session and seeing clients in the hospital or in their homes if necessary.

11. HSP should live in the community, particularly if the center is in a rural area. Human services internships, sponsored by universities, could be explored as an alternative for staffing centers in rural areas. In addition, community members should be trained as paraprofessionals. The center should also provide folk healing and religious mental health services if necessary.

12. The therapeutic modalities used should be determined on an individual basis. Pluralistic counseling and psychotherapy can be used as a general framework in conjunction with other indigenous approaches.

13. The center should develop brochures and use the media to advertise its services. In the United States, advertising should be in both Spanish and English. In Latin American countries, advertising should be in Spanish and the indigenous language of the population to which services would be provided.

14. HSP and community members should "trumpet" their accomplishment. A big "fiesta" should celebrate the establishment of the center and the cooperative work done by HSP and the community.

15. Implementation of services should always include community members. Monthly meetings with the community advisory committee should be held to continuously determine if the center is meeting the needs of the people.

16. A yearly program evaluation should be conducted to determine how the program is doing. Satisfaction of community members and HSP should be assessed.

17. The program evaluation serves as a basis for future needs assessment projects, which should be conducted every 3 to 5 years to determine if needs are being met or if needs are changing.

Needs assessment and service delivery in human service areas are difficult and complex projects. They can be especially difficult in rural areas, where residents often distrust urbanites. Nevertheless, it is important that HSP reach out to all sectors of the population and all types of communities in order to improve counseling and human development services for Latin Americans.

References

Abad, V., Ramos, J., & Boyce, E. (1974). A model for delivery of mental health services to Spanish-speaking minorities. *American Journal of Orthopsychiatry, 44*, 584–595.

Acosta, X. F., & Cristo, M. H. (1981). Development of a bilingual interpreter program: An alternative model for Spanish-speaking services. *Professional Psychology, 21*, 474–481.

Acosta, X. F., Evans, L. A., Hurwicz, M. L., & Yamamoto, J. (1987). In M. Gaviria & J. D. Arana (Eds.), *Health and behavior: Research agenda for Hispanics.* Chicago, IL: Simon Bolivar Hispanic-American Psychiatric Research and Training Program.

Alarcon, R. D. (1986). La salud mental en America Latina, 1970–1985 (Mental health in Latin America, 1970–1985). *Boletin de la Oficina Sanitaria Panamericana, 101*, 567–592.

Cohen, M. W. (1976). A simplified method for selecting dwelling units for a household survey. *Journal of Community Psychology, 4*, 124–129.

Flaming, K. H. (1976). Assessing community self-studies: A comment on a simplified method of selecting dwelling units for a household survey. *Journal of Community Psychology, 4*, 130–136.

Gonzales, R. U. (1976). Salud mental en America Latina: Problemas y perspectivas (Mental health in Latin America: Problems and perspectives). *Boletin de la Oficina Sanitaria Panamericana, 81*, 93–108.

Humm-Delgado, D., & Delgado, M. (1983). Assessing Hispanic mental health needs: Issues and recommendations. *Journal of Community Psychology, 11*, 363–375.

Humm-Delgado, D., & Delgado, M. (1986). Gaining community entree to assess services needs of Hispanics. *Social Casework: The Journal of Contemporary Social Work, 67*, 80–89.

Hurst, M., & Zambrana, R. E. (1980). The health careers of urban women: A study of East Harlem. *Journal of Women in Culture and Society, 5*, 112–126.

Josephson, E. (1970). Resistance to community surveys. *Social Problems, 18*, 117–129.

Keefe, S. E. (1979). Mexican-Americans' underutilization of mental health clinics: An evaluation of suggested explanations. *Hispanic Journal of Behavioral Sciences, 1*, 93–115.

LeVine, E. S., & Padilla, A. M. (1980). *Crossing cultures in therapy: Pluralistic counseling for the Hispanic*. Monterey, CA: Brooks/Cole.

Marcos, L. R. (1976). Bilinguals in psychotherapy: Language as an emotional barrier. *American Journal of Psychotherapy, 30*, 552–559.

Normand, W. C., Inglesias, J., & Payn, S. (1974). Brief group therapy to facilitate utilization of mental health services by Spanish-speaking patients. *American Journal of Orthopsychiatry, 44*, 37–42.

Padilla, A. M. (1980). *Acculturation: Theory, models and some new findings*. Boulder, CO: American Association for the Advancement of Science.

Padilla, A. M. (1981). Pluralistic counseling and psychotherapy for Hispanic Americans. In A. J. Marsella & P. B. Pedersen (Eds.), *Cross-cultural counseling and psychotherapy* (pp. 195–227). New York: Pergamon Press.

Padilla, A. M., Ruiz, R. A., & Alvarez, R. (1975). Community mental health services for the Spanish-speaking/surnamed population. *American Psychologist, 30*, 892–905.

Peroto, P. C. (1975). Psicoterapia en Bolivia: Necesidad o despilfarro? (Psychotherapy in Bolivia: Necessity or waste?). *Revista Interamericana de Psicologia, 9*, 105–109.

Phillips, M. J. (1971). Successful and unsuccessful approaches to mental health services for an urban Hispano-American population. *Journal of Public Health, 61*, 820–830.

Pine, G. J. (1972). Counseling minority groups: A review of the literature. *Counseling and Values, 17*, 35–44.

Rosado, J. W. (1980). Important psychocultural factors in the delivery of mental health services to lower-class Puerto Rican clients: A review of recent studies. *Journal of Community Psychology, 61*, 215–226.

Ruiz, E. J. (1975). Influence of bilingualism communication in groups. *International Journal of Group Psychotherapy, 25*, 391–395.

Ruiz, R. A., & Casas, J. M. (1981). Culturally relevant and behavioristic counseling for Chicano college students. In P. B. Pedersen, J. G. Draguns, W. J. Lonner, & J. E. Trimble (Eds.), *Counseling across cultures*. Honolulu: University of Hawaii Press.

Ruiz, R. A., & Padilla, A. M. (1977). Counseling Latinos. *Personnel and Guidance Journal, 55*, 401–408.

Ryan, R. A. (1980). The community perspective for mental health research. *Social Casework, 61*, 507–511.

Sue, D. W. (1977). Counseling the culturally different: A conceptual analysis. *Personnel and Guidance Journal, 55*, 422–425.

Sue, D. W. (1981). *Counseling the culturally different: Theory and practice.* New York: Wiley.

Torrey, E. F. (1972). *The mind game: Witchdoctors and psychiatrists.* New York: Emerson Hall.

Tsung-Yi Lin. (1984). Mental health and the third world—challenges and hope: The Margaret Mead memorial lecture. In R. C. Nann, D. D. Butt, & L. Ladrido Ignacio (Eds.), *Mental health, cultural values, and social development: A look into the 80's.* Boston: Reidel.

Vasquez, A. G., & Uhlig, G. E. (1978). The Spanish-speaking of Chicago: Social service issues. *Social Perspectives, 6*, 25–29.

Velasquez, J. S., & Velasquez, C. P. (1980). Applications of a bicultural assessment framework to social work practice with Hispanics. *Family Relations, 29*, 598–603.

Velez, C. G. (1980). Mexicano/Hispano support systems and confianza: Theoretical issues of cultural adaptation. In R. Valle & W. Vega (Eds.), *Hispanic natural support systems: Mental health promotion perspective.* California: California Department of Mental Health.

A Needs Assessment of Hispanic Students at a Predominantly White University

Jairo Fuertes, William E. Sedlacek, and Franklin D. Westbrook

Abstract

The authors provide the results of a pilot study conducted to assess the extent to which Latino/ Hispanic students at a large northeastern university in the United States become involved in activities and ethnic organizations, feel that they have special needs at the university, and identify with the university and the minority student office. Based on personal interviews with 10 students and responses to a questionnaire from 150 randomly selected Latino/Hispanic students, the authors discuss the within-group differences of Latino/Hispanic students and offer recommendations for improving services to this population on campus.

Resumen

Los autores dan los resultados de un estudio piloto dirigido para calcular hasta qué punto los estudiantes latinohispánicos en una universidad noreste grande en los Estados Unidos se involucren en actividades y en organizaciones étnicas, crean que ellos tienen necesidades especiales en la universidad, e identifiquen con la universidad y la oficina estudiantil de minoría. Basado en unas entrevistas personales con 10 estudiantes y las respuestas a un cuestionario de 150 estudiantes latinohispánicos seleccionados sin orden, los autores discuten las diferencias dentro del grupo de estudiantes latinohispánicos y ofrecen recomendaciones para mejorar los servicios a esta población al campo.

Introduction

In the last 30 years minorities have increasingly enrolled in predominantly White universities (Fleming, 1984). Enrollment data for the decade of the 1980s show that four out of every five minority students enrolled in higher education attend predominantly White colleges and universities (Livingston & Stewart, 1987). However, it has been difficult for minority students at such schools to adjust academically and socially to campus life (Garza & Nelson, 1973; Hunt, 1975; Lyon, 1973; Olivas, 1982; Sedlacek, 1987). Minority groups have reported not feeling welcome on traditionally White campuses (Parker & Scott, 1985).

The task of understanding the situation of minority students in predominantly White universities is becoming more complex. Minorities have been shown to differ in their aspirations and expectations of college life (Minatoya & Sedlacek, 1984), and in what they identify as their main problems in higher education (Westbrook, Miyares, & Roberts, 1978; Webster, Sedlacek, & Miyares, 1979). However, research on minorities has often combined different minority groups for the purpose of analyzing and interpreting their responses. Those doing assessments have ignored the needs of particular minority groups (Keller, Piotrowski, & Sherry, 1982). Therefore, the purpose of this study was to assess specifically the extent to which Hispanic students at a large northeastern university become involved in activities and ethnic organizations, feel that they have special needs at the university, and identify with the university and the minority student office on campus.

Method

The needs assessment consisted of two parts. The first part involved interviews with 10 randomly selected Hispanic students chosen from groups of successful and unsuccessful students; 5 students with grade point averages (GPAs) below 2.0, and 5 students with GPAs of 3.2 and above. The second part of the needs assessment was the administration of a 28-item questionnaire developed on the basis of interview results. The questionnaire was mailed to 150 randomly selected Hispanic students and 109 (75%) were returned.

Results

Of the respondents, 44% were men, 54% women (2% unspecified), 25% freshmen, 25% sophomores, 28% juniors, 21% seniors, and 1% "other." Twenty-eight percent lived on campus, 56% off campus with family, 14% off campus with others, and 2% off campus alone. Sixty-three percent were born in the United States, 7% belonged to a Hispanic organization on campus, and 35% belonged to a non-Hispanic organization on campus.

A comparison of student responses showed that male Hispanics living on campus had more time for student groups than those living off campus with their families. Hispanics who belonged to non-Hispanic groups felt it was important to participate in student groups, and that they had more time to participate in them. They felt that minority student groups should provide Hispanics academic and financial support rather than political or cultural awareness.

Hispanics who were not involved in non-Hispanic groups felt that they had special needs on campus. The main reasons Hispanics gave for failing in school were financial or motivational concerns. Interestingly, 86% of the respondents had heard of the minority student office on campus, but 73% said that they had not used its services. Hispanics wanted to know more about the minority office, and they wanted this office to take greater interest in Hispanics.

Pearson correlations showed that the more years students had spent in the United States the more likely they were to feel a sense of belonging at the university ($r = -.30$, $p<.05$) and the more non-Hispanic friends they had on campus ($r=.25$, $p<.05$). Also, the more time they had spent in the United States, the less interest they had in the minority student office's involvement with Hispanic students ($r = .20$, $p < .05$), and the less likely they were to have Hispanic friends ($r = .30$, $p < .05$). As the number of years spent in the United States increased, Hispanics were more likely to say that they had no special needs at the university ($r = .17$, $p < .05$).

Discussion

Hispanics who feel it is important to be involved in campus activities seem to be able to find groups that will accept them. However, a large number of Hispanics (58%) felt that it was not important to join organizations. Sedlacek (1987) showed that campus/community activity is important for minority student success at predominantly White institutions. Incoming Hispanic students ought to be informed (at orientation, for example) about the importance of being involved on campus. Hispanic students who are active in school are more likely to develop a sense of belonging on campus, develop friendships with support persons in their college, and meet appropriate role models.

Hispanics living off campus reported having little time for campus activities and organizations. These students may not be getting as much information or encouragement from the university or their families to get involved on campus (Quevedo-Garcia, 1987). Conversely, students living on campus probably have greater access to information about activities and organizations than students living off campus. They may also be more encouraged by their peers to join or participate in groups and activities.

Hispanics who join non-Hispanic groups on campus are less likely to feel that Hispanics have special needs on campus. It seems that students who join non-Hispanic groups find themselves in the mainstream. In contrast, Hispanic students who do not join non-Hispanic groups may perceive a culture gap and may prefer to join or create Hispanic organizations. These groups may help Hispanics meet the need for affiliation and representation. Support units ought to be aware of these needs and be ready to help Hispanics organize their own groups.

Evidence that students know the minority student office exists and think it is important, yet choose not to use it, may seem surprising. However, Schneider (1987) showed that environments tend to be shaped by the predominant groups that inhabit them, and they discourage those that are different. Because Hispanics are not the largest minority group on the campus where this study was conducted, and the minority student office is not staffed by Hispanics, Hispanic students may feel that the office is not responsive to their needs. Results of this study show that Hispanics wanted to know more about the minority student office and wanted this office to take greater interest in them. The minority student office should ensure that its programs and staff recognize the special needs of Hispanics.

Another reason Hispanics do not utilize the services of the minority student office may be that as they acculturate to the majority culture, their attitudes and perceptions of the college environment become more like those of Whites (Born, 1970; Padilla, Alvarez, & Lindholm, 1986). Future research concerning Hispanics could examine the effects of acculturation, specifically to explain how it affects Hispanic students' help-seeking behaviors in college.

References

Born, D. (1970). Psychological adaptation and development under acculturative stress: Toward a general model. *Social Science and Medicine, 3,* 529–547.

Fleming, J. (1984). *Blacks in college*. San Francisco: Jossey-Bass.

Garza, R. T., & Nelson, E. B. (1973). A comparison of Mexican and Anglo-American student perceptions of the university environment. *Journal of College Student Personnel, 14*, 399–401.

Hunt, C. L. (1975). Alternate patterns of minority group adjustment in the university. *Education Forum, 39*, 137–147.

Keller, J., Piotrowsky, C., & Sherry, D. (1982). Perceptions of the college environment and campus life: The Black experience. *Journal of Non-White Concerns in Personnel and Guidance, 10*, 126–132.

Livingston, M. D., & Stewart, M. A. (1987). Minority students on a White campus: Perception is truth. *National Association of Student Personnel Administrators Journal, 24*, 38–49.

Lyon, J. E. (1973). The adjustment of Black students to a predominantly White campus. *Journal of Negro Education, 42*, 462–466.

Minatoya, L. Y., & Sedlacek, W. E. (1984). Assessing attitudes of White university students toward Blacks in a changing context. *Journal of Non-White Concerns in Personnel and Guidance, 12*, 69–79.

Olivas, M. A. (1982). Federal higher education policy: The case of Hispanics. *Educational Evaluation and Policy Analysis, 4*, 301–310.

Padilla, A., Alvarez, M., & Lindholm, K. J. (1986). Generational and personality factors as predictors of stress in students. *Hispanic Journal of Behavioral Sciences, 8*, 275–288.

Parker, W. P., & Scott, A. C. (1985). Creating an inviting atmosphere for college students from ethnic minority groups. *Journal of College Student Personnel, 26*, 82–87.

Quevedo-Garcia, E. L. (1987). Facilitating the development of Hispanic college students. In D. J. Wright (Ed.), *Responding to the needs of today's minority students* (pp. 49–63). New Directions for Student Services, No. 38. San Francisco: Jossey-Bass.

Schneider, B. (1987). E = f (P,B): The road to a radical approach to Person-Evironment fit. *Journal of Vocational Behavior, 31*, 353–361.

Sedlacek, W. E. (1987). Black students on White campuses: 20 years of research. *Journal of College Student Personnel, 28*(6), 484–495.

Webster, D. W., Sedlacek, W. E., & Miyares, J. (1979). A comparison of problems perceived by minority and White students. *Journal of College Student Personnel, 20*, 165–170.

Westbrook, F. D., Miyares, J., & Roberts, J. (1978). Perceived problem areas by Black and White students and hints about comparative counseling needs. *Journal of Counseling Psychology, 25*, 131–136.

PART III

COMMUNICATION

Good communication is the essence of meaningful cross-cultural interaction. Through effective communication, counseling and human development specialists can help remove barriers to dialogue between and within culturally different groups. However, good cross-cultural communication requires more than an understanding of language; it requires, among other things, an understanding of cultural values, respect for differences, sensitivity to self, knowledge of group dymamics, and nonverbal communication skills. Effective communication with Latino/Hispanic groups can open avenues of resources and opportunities for greater understanding and positive development across cultures.

In part 3 of this monograph, Johnnie Miles presents a plenary paper focused on a model of cross-cultural communication that transcends simple spoken language. She gives special emphasis to the role of counseling and the role of the counselor in addressing social issues and fostering meaningful intercultural and interracial exchange. In the paper that follows, David Whitfield discusses a model of counselor training designed to enhance multicultural counseling skills. Finally, Carlos Heredia presents results of his research dealing with the influence of ethnic background on bilingual (Spanish-English) Columbians and Anglo-American college students on perceived counselor expertness.

PLENARY ADDRESS

THE ROLE OF THE COUNSELOR IN INTERCULTURAL AND INTERRACIAL EXCHANGE

Johnnie H. Miles

Abstract

The author discusses the special role of counseling and the role of the counselor in addressing social issues and fostering intercultural and interracial exchange. The potential negative impact of the counselor who holds stereotypical attitudes or lacks cultural knowledge is highlighted. Several examples and case histories of counselors dealing with cross-cultural situations are used to illustrate important points. In conclusion, the author points out that counselors should call upon their "healer's nature" to empower clients and affect systems.

Resumen

La autora discute el papel especial de consejar y el papel del consejero/de la consejera en dirigirse a las cuestiones sociales y en fomentar intercambio intercultural e interracial. Se subraya el impacto potencialmente negativo del consejero/de la consejera que tenga actitudes estereotípicas o que carezca del conocimiento cultural. Se utilizan varios ejemplos e historias clínicas de consejeros que se ocupan con situaciones de cruzamiento de culturas para ilustrar puntos importantes. En conclusión, la autora señala que los consejeros deben reclamar su "naturaleza de curador/a" para dar poder a clientes y para afectar sistemas.

Introduction

The focus of this paper is on communication as it relates to the role of counseling and the role of the counselor in addressing social issues and fostering intercultural and interracial exchange. It will begin with some stories I heard recently. One of these stories is an experience that a politician related, and the other came from a story told at a recent AACD convention. What do these two professionals, a counselor and a politician, and their stories have in common? As you will see, in many ways they have collaborated over the years, unbeknownst to each other in most cases, in setting social policy that has dictated much of what we do in counseling today.

A U.S. senator who was speaking about why he was in politics and why he had aligned himself with a particular political party recounted this story: He said that he was listening to a debate between two national candidates in a recent election who were responding to reporters who had asked the question about their prior record and what they had done to deal with the homeless. One candidate spoke up rather quickly and in elaborate detail laid out his message. He said that one day while talking about his busy schedule, he realized that he needed to take some time for himself. He took 2 hours. Two hours were hard to come by, and he went down to a local homeless shelter where he took the time to shake hands and to talk with the people who were there. The senator indicated that he was taken aback by the comment of that candidate. He said that he had always known on an intellectual level why he had chosen his own profession, but it was at that moment that he truly understood why he had chosen his career. The senator said that he was there because those people are our people. They are us. They are as I am and you are. They are an intricate part of humanity. Regardless of the state of life that has befallen us, we are as one. And we deserve to be given equal protection and opportunity under every system of the land. And he said further, "I do what I do because I care, and because I care, I have chosen a profession that carries with it the responsibility to care for others."

The other story was an experience that took place at the recent convention of the American Association for Counseling and Development in Cincinnati. The theme for that conference was Global Vision—Celebrating Diversity and Creating Community. On Sunday morning, the day before the close of the convention, there was an early morning presentation on that theme made by a renowned professor from Georgia State by the name of Asa Grant Hilliat. He started his presentation by quoting an East African writer, I. E. Oquoy Omar, who wrote a book entitled *The Healers*. The book recounts a conversation between a healer and a passerby on the criteria for a person going into training to be a healer. Hilliat had translated "healer" from the East African perspective into counselor or psychologist or psychiatrist. He used the following quote: "After the training, the healer walks through the same world that others walk through but he sees signs that others don't see. Hears sounds that others don't hear. The same tree that just stands there dumbly to everyone, to the healer its leaves have things to say. The healer learns the meaning of the river sounds, the sounds of the forest animals, and when he needs the curing spirit from a plant, if his eyes are well prepared, he may see from a great distance some small sign of the leaf that is ready to be taken." And so the passerby said, "Can everyone be a healer?" And the healer answered "No." "Well, why not?" asked the passerby. And the healer said, "A healer must first have a healer's nature, and I can't tell you what it is just so, but for a beginning, he who would be a healer must set great value on seeing truly, hearing truly, understanding truly, and acting truly." The healer laughed at himself and he said, "You see now why healing can't be a popular vocation, because the healer would rather see and hear and understand than have power over men, and most people you see would rather have power over men than to hear or see."

Think about the people who provide services under the guise of counseling as being unique. It even becomes an expectation that those people be special. In counseling books, when you get to the section in the textbook where all of the characteristics for successful helping are listed, students are overwhelmed because they say, "I fall so far short of that."

When one takes on the role of a counselor, he or she must take on the challenge and responsibility of responding to clients' needs, performing whatever tasks are necessary through whatever means possible. If, as the politician says, your profession calls for you to care, and counseling certainly does, then care you must. The counselor is or should be a special person. A counselor must have a depth of understanding, a vision of what is possible, a belief in a person's ability to change, and a commitment to serve that takes him or her into a special realm of relating and service.

To be a counselor in the 1990s offers an opportunity to be all of the above and more. We live in a complex world, a world that is global, and right now distance is not even a dividing factor. And we live in a society that is multicultural. Our society has always been culturally diverse; now in the 1990s we are taking a new look at the concept of multiculturalism. More specifically, we are considering the role of counselors and the role of the profession in working within a multicultural environment.

Paul Pedersen has been critical of the fact that sometimes our ideas about cultural diversity are narrow—we think about people being only African-American, or Hispanic, or Asian, and we limit it to that. In fact, he says, every time you enter a counseling relationship there is a high probability that diversity will play a role. Whether that diversity comes from racial, ethnic, or cultural differences, or whether it comes from age and race or class or even gender issues, it is likely to be there. And so, as professionals, we need to broaden our concept of what cultural diversity means.

We know that, in counseling, establishing a good working relationship with a client is a real challenge, even if you are as much like the client as possible. It is a real challenge when you encounter diversity. But the diversity that comes from racial, ethnic, and cultural aspects, perhaps because we understand it the least, presents the greatest challenge of all. If we're going to learn to understand each other, it must come from in-depth study and interaction.

In discussing Spanish-speaking cultures, one approach could be to discuss history, heterogeneity, immigration patterns, assimilation and acculturation stress, the importance of the family, problems with language, religion, health-related issues, stereotyped traditions, and values. We could focus on the end result of some of these things: the impact of the stereotypes and the impact of counselors' lack of knowledge. To illustrate this latter point, I will present three actual case studies.

Case Studies

To interpret the case studies, the following questions are suggested: What happened in the case? What were the social issues involved in the case? Were they individual issues or were they collective issues directed at a specific group? To what extent were cultural components or variables overlooked? Was it an intercultural exchange or interaction? To what extent could consideration of cultural variables have made a difference in the counseling process?

The first case is that of a 16-year-old 10th grader from Puerto Rico. Juan moved stateside with his family 2 years ago so that his family, who had been out of work in Puerto Rico, could find a job. Although his father was highly skilled in the building trades, he had been unable to find a job when he moved to the States because it was very hard to break into the unions. He could speak broken English but, at the same time, he could understand a lot more than what he could speak. The only work the father had been able to find was in janitorial services. Although it was a low-paying, dead-end job, it was a job nevertheless. But it did not allow the family to live at the level they had hoped. So the mother had to go to work. The father turned to drinking heavily, fights between the parents escalated, and sometimes the fights spilled over into conflicts between Juan and his father. At school Juan was getting average grades, although his test scores were well below average. Juan's English was not perfect. Whenever he would mispronounce a word or would use improper grammar, he was teased. Juan had a great deal of tolerance and he would take a lot. But when he reached his saturation level he would strike out at others. Juan had three male classmates who were always involved in these altercations with him. So, whenever they would have fights, the teacher would take them in tow to the assistant principal, who had the responsibility for discipline. The first time this occurred the assistant principal did the usual kind of thing and read the student handbook to them about violence on school premises and gave them a minilecture and sent them back to class with a warning—"Don't do it again." The second time the teacher arrived with the four in tow, the assistant principal sent the other three students back to class, but he sent Juan to a counselor instead. He sent a sealed note to the counselor that said: "I want you to talk with this young man because I see in him some sullen, resistant kind of hostile behavior, and let's see if we can nip this in the bud." In his interaction with Juan, the counselor confirmed the assistant principal's view and chalked it all up to Juan's attempt at being macho. The third encounter occurred 1 month later when the three students confronted Juan on the school grounds after school. Juan held his own. His small stature did not work against him and the three received the worst of the altercation. When it was stopped, those three young men were ushered off to see the school nurse, they were suspended for 3 days, and Juan was also suspended for 3 days. He was accused of having a knife, although there were no scars on the three young men. Nor was there a knife at the scene that could be tied to Juan. But he was suspended nevertheless for 3 days.

The second case is that of Maria. Maria is a 22-year-old young woman from Mexico. She was a new participant in a manpower employment training and counseling program designed to prepare individuals for a job search. Maria had learned about the program while she was enrolled in an evening adult education English class. Her teacher had talked with her a little bit about the program and she decided to enroll in it. Midway through the program, she was talking to one of the counselors about the difficulty in finding good child care. She was worried about what that was going to mean for her if and when she found a job. She was also heartbroken because she was going through this program and did not feel ready to go to work, at least not right away, the reason being that she was pregnant again. Maria already has four children, all under 6 years of age. Although she was happy about her pregnancy, she realized that she could not go to work. The counselor was angry with Maria because she couldn't understand how Maria allowed herself to get pregnant. The counselor wondered what kind of birth control she was using and whether she had considered having an abortion. The counselor proceeded to probe these issues with Maria and, as a result, Maria grew quiet and nonresponsive. The session was soon over, and Maria never returned to counseling and left the manpower program before completion.

The third case is that of Rosa, a 15-year-old Cuban student who moved to the United States some 6 years ago. She is described as outgoing, has many friends, mostly Anglo, is a good student, and is being considered for the gifted and talented program at her school next year. She is active in extracurricular activities like the debate club and drama. She is well liked by students and staff. She was described recently by one of her teachers as an all-American kid. Rosa has two older brothers, 17 and 19, and one sister, who is 12. Recently, Rosa has had numerous conflicts with her parents because she wanted to spend more time with her friends. She wanted to date more and she wanted to be able to stay out later like her friends. She became very critical of her parents for holding on to what she thought were old-fashioned ideas and for speaking Spanish at home. And so she began to resist participating in family events. Rosa's brothers became very critical of Rosa, especially about her behavior at school. The parents thought Rosa was not a good role model for her sister. Rosa referred herself to counseling, wanting to figure out how she could keep herself from going crazy by being pulled in different directions by all these various people. The counselor began to work with Rosa on becoming more assertive with her brothers, and expressing her views better with her parents. They also talked about issues of growing up, maturing and being more independent, and separation from family.

Now let's go back and review each of these cases. In reviewing Juan's case, the social issues were unemployment, drug and alcohol abuse, dysfunctional behavior in the family, and perhaps even emotional and physical abuse. Interpersonal relationship issues with his peers, racism, discrimination, and inequitable treatment were also important concerns. Certainly the counselor's lack of cultural awareness and sensitivity was a factor. Would the counselor have been better able to work with Juan if he had known more about Puerto Rican history, racism, and oppression? Would he have been more open and responsive if he had seen that situation as discriminatory and racist? Would he have understood more if he could have identified the inequitable treatment? What would the counselor have needed to know to be able to see those larger issues?

Maria's situation also involved unemployment and all the intervening variables associated with that problem. There were issues of religious practices and values as well. Would it have helped the counselor to know that Maria was a long-time practicing Catholic? Would it have been helpful for her to know that Maria was living in an area where she was not surrounded by Hispanic families and friends to use as resources? And would the counselor have been better off if she had acknowledged Maria's dilemma and helped Maria to identify resources from the church and from other areas in the school?

Rosa's case is very different from the previous two. Here you see a successful student by anybody's standards, but a student in conflict, nevertheless. The counselor saw her as being too externally motivated, as lacking assertiveness, and as needing knowledge about normal developmental issues of teenagers. Is that so? Could it be that Rosa was dealing with acculturation stress resulting from trying to assimilate into a new culture?

Fortunately, for Maria, Rosa, and others, our trend as counselors is moving away from forcing people into set patterns. We are beginning to dispell some mistaken notions about acculturation and about counseling clients fom different cultures. We are moving more toward acceptance of the concept of pluralism with ethnic identity in counseling. Central to this concept is the idea that people are healthier when they know their roots. That is, if they know who they are and feel good about who they are, it is so much easier to accept and feel good about other people. In many ways, feeling good about oneself forms the basis for positive egalitarian exchanges.

Conclusion

Members of the counseling profession can no longer ignore the inefficacy of using monocultural approaches with multicultural clientele. There is a need for approaches with pluralistic perspectives to accommodate a wide range of individual and group differences. Although approaches designed from a cross-cultural perspective are emerging, progress has been slow. The profession can stimulate that process by calling for research and development of multicultural approaches. One place to start this research is to learn what other cultures do. So many cultures have been able successfully to handle the kinds of concerns and problems we see in mental health issues, and they don't even use the word "counseling." What do they have that we can use? What can we learn from the Puerto Ricans and their concept of espiritismo? What can we learn from the African cultures and their counsel of elders, or their notion of medicine men and women and healers?

Counseling is a profession that cares and helps. Those who are drawn to it are special people by nature; a healer's nature in the counseling profession calls counselors to be advocates, it calls counselors to be activists, it calls counselors to empower clients. And when I'm talking about empowering clients, I am talking about helping them to accept who they are and to accept others. People should be taught how systems work, so that if systems are not meeting their needs, they will know enough to change those systems. In order to do that job, however, counselors must be culturally sensitive. Counselors should really think about who they are and the culture from whence they come; they must focus first on who they are before they can understand other people and promote an equal exchange.

How to Improve Multicultural Counseling

Abstract

The author offers a definition of multicultural counseling and presents a model designed to train counselors along seven specific dimensions of multicultural counseling. Using a taxonomy made up of knowledge, comprehension, application, analysis, synthesis, and evaluation, the model provides a framework for the counselor educator and the counseling student to move in a direction of greater cultural sensitivity along the seven dimensions of multicultural counseling proposed. The author suggests that this taxonomy offers an excellent way to measure both faculty and counseling student progress in becoming literate and competent in other cultures.

Resumen

El autor ofrece una definición de los consejos multiculturales y presenta un modelo diseñado para adiestrar a los consejeros por siete dimensiones específicas de los consejos multiculturales. Utilizando una taxonomía compuesta del conocimiento, la comprensión, la aplicación, el análisis, la síntesis, y la evaluación, el modelo ofrece un marco para que el educador-consejero/la educadora-consejera y el/la estudiante consejero/a mueva en una dirección de mayor sensibilidad cultural a lo largo de las siete dimensiones de los consejos multiculturales propuestas. El autor sugiere que esta taxonomía ofrezca un modo excelente de medir tanto el progreso de la facultad como el del/de la estudiante consejero/a al llegar a ser culto/a y capaz en otras culturas.

Introduction

Using the following dimensions, how would a counselor educator help move a counseling student toward the right on each?

From (a/an)	Toward (a/an)
Monolingual Counselor	Multilingual Counselor
Monocultural View	Multicultural View
Multiculturally Illiterate	Multiculturally Literate
Ethnically Uninformed	Ethnically Informed
Ecologically Illiterate	Ecologically Literate
Passive Counselor	Active Counselor
Subjective Counselor	Objective Counselor

Before discussing the use of the above dimensions and how to use them as yardsticks to measure counseling students' progress in multicultural learning, perhaps it is best to address specific questions and have a brief look at some of the more recent literature concerning multicultural counseling.

What is multicultural counseling? What are some attributes of a multicultural counselor? What should a counselor know about another culture to be an effective helper? How does a counselor enter, for example, the Hispanic culture or other cultures? What is an effective approach to help counselor trainees become more literate in other cultures? How may counselors become competent in cultures of diversified racial, religious, sexual, and ethnic groups?

This paper addresses the above questions and suggests ways of becoming an intentional (Ivey & Simek-Downing, 1980), more mature multicultural counselor. But before addressing the above questions, a suggested definition of multicultural counseling follows.

Multicultural Counseling: A Suggested Definition

Until there is a clear and accepted definition of multicultural counseling, counselor educators will continue to teach counselors to help others in their monocultural shroud. Ponterotto and Casas (1987) alluded to a definition that includes knowledge and skills, and suggest a more comprehensive, inclusive definition of multicultural counseling. It includes: the delivery of services to persons or groups of persons who differ culturally, ethnically, sexually, religiously, ecologically, and educationally. This also includes knowledge of the client's culture and its language, music, literature, history, and ecological variables.

In following this suggested definition, a key question is: Do we want to know the culture or do we want to know about the culture? How this question is answered will set the direction of multiculturally competent counselor preparation. Specifically, if on the one hand we want to know the culture, then we must live in that culture: get an apartment in the barrio or in the ghetto, live in it and experience some of the ecological frustrations that, for example, Hispanics, Blacks, Asian Americans, and other culturally different groups must endure daily. On the other hand, if we want to know about the culture, we can do it at a distance, which may not be as effective as living in the culture. It is not realistic, however, to expect every counselor to live in another culture.

If the above suggested definition of multicultural counseling is accepted, then what are some attributes of a multicultural counselor? A suggested response is a counselor who: (a) is literate in different cultures; (b) has a tolerance for uncertainty and ambiguity; (c) is flexible, sensitive, open-minded, and empathic; and (d) has tolerance for confusion.

Considering these attributes, to counsel a Hispanic or a Black effectively, for example, a counselor should read such works as: *Down These Mean Streets*; *Black Boy*; *Chicano*; *Native Son*; *My Soul is Rested*; *If Beale Street Could Talk*; *Go Tell it on the Mountain Top*; *Invisible Man*; or similar works. Such reading will help the counselor to understand the psychology of the culture or persons being counseled and become more tolerant of members of different cultures.

What should a counselor know about another culture? A counselor should at least be familiar with the language, literature, history, music, values, and ecology of another culture, familiar enough to apply that knowledge to engender in the client of that culture a desire, psychologically, to "buy into" what the counselor is delivering. By knowing about these variables, a counselor can better understand the expectation of, for example, a Hispanic client, or how she or he sees the world. Counselors who have a knowledge deficit of other cultures may need retooling. Just as the plateaued manager needs retooling (Whitfield, 1989), counselors also need retooling to counsel persons from different cultures, unless they have been trained specifically to do so.

We must be careful, however, not to assume that everyone who is culturally different wants to be treated differently therapeutically. Ivey supported this notion when he stated: "Counseling skills and techniques are to be used differently with different groups, but within each group is immense individual variation" (Ivey, 1987, p. 169). This is analogous to an organization; namely, counseling skills that work in one organizational setting may totally fail in another (Whitfield, 1989). The same applies to counseling culturally different groups or individuals.

The literature is fraught with such antediluvian terms as *minority* and *majority*. These terms are corroded; they have a certain corrosive ubiquity; they have served their time and are worn out, given the statistic that seven eighths of the world is non-White. Besides, this type of labeling impedes counselor and counselor educator effectiveness. These terms should be stricken from the literature, the curricula, and the counselor vocabulary.

The literature is bountiful with references about Hispanics' and Blacks' ending counseling prematurely, at the rate of 50% as compared with 30% for Whites (Watson, 1983). Why? One explanation is that the counselor does not know how these clients see the world and vice versa. Another explanation, as Watson pointed out, is that "many minority clients receive ineffective counseling due to inadequate preparation of their counselors" (Watson, p. 5). Additionally, culturally different persons do not psychologically buy into what the counselor is selling.

Herr supported this when he stated: "Fundamental counseling and therapeutic principles are not absolute and unswervingly waiting for discovery and dealt with by helpers who are capable of interpretation and reflection" (Herr, 1989, p. 31). As Ivey pointed out, however, multicultural counseling should be the core of counseling (Ivey, 1987). Without this attitude toward multicultural counseling, counselors will continue to counsel in a monocultural mode, a practice the United States or England can ill-afford.

When counselors ignore cultural differences, they: (a) deprive clients of their identity; (b) they consign themselves to superficiality and reification of a problem that is perhaps kaleidoscopic for the client. Without some knowledge of a client's culture, counselors will in all probability find themselves in creative silence, followed by psychobabble void of substance. This, too, is supported by Ivey: "Workshops in the Canadian Arctic with the Navajo and other Native American groups, and research on women and Blacks . . . all led to the awareness that microskills and therapy without multicultural concerns and cultural expertise were empty and hollow" (Ivey, 1987, p. 169).

Russell stated that "before considering how to educate, it is well to be clear as to the sort of result which we wish to achieve" (Russell, 1985, p. 5). When applied properly, Bloom's taxonomy is an effective tool that not only provides what is to be achieved but also suggests ways of achieving results and becoming competent in other cultures. To paraphrase Biehler, this taxonomy is a comprehensive classification of goals that counselor educators should try to achieve in their efforts to produce multiculturally competent counselors.

The dimensions cited above may be used by educational institutions as yardsticks to measure counseling students' progress in learning to become literate and competent in other cultures. But are counseling faculty prepared to teach multicultural material? These yardsticks may help counseling faculty to prepare themselves and their students. This issue is similar to computer illiterate faculty preparing to teach students who want to become computer-literate or who are already computer-literate (Whitfield, 1984). Namely, are counseling faculty multiculturally literate enough to teach counseling students who want to become literate and competent in other cultures?

Improving Multicultural Competence

To increase useful knowledge about other cultures, Bloom's taxonomy of Educational Objectives (Biehler, 1974), in combination with the andragogical approach (Knowles, 1980) is offered. This approach is pertinent in this context because it compartmentalizes information in such a manner that the counselor trainee or learner can see at any given point where she or he is. It also affords the opportunity to build on what information is attained. It is not a recipe etched in stone, but rather a solid foundation on which to build. The andragogical part of the method suggests self-directedness on the part of the counseling student.

In applying this taxonomy, the counselor educator and counseling students may conjointly construct a list of mind openers that both feel the counseling student may want to consider in order to be effective in a multicultural setting. This would help in moving the counseling student from a monocultural view toward a multicultural view. This is in harmony with the andragogical approach (Knowles, 1980), which is the art and science of helping adults learn, as compared to pedagogy, which is the art and science of teaching children. The relationship between teacher and student under the andragogical model is that of facilitator and colearner. By doing the mind openers together, both educator and counseling student will create richer, more comprehensive lists of what is to be learned about other cultures.

Bloom classifies the objectives into three domains (Biehler, 1974): cognitive, affective, and psychomotor. But for lack of space, let's use an abridged portion of Bloom's condensed version of the educational objectives, which subsumes the cognitive domain. By starting with the first objective, knowledge, we can help move a counseling student, along the first dimension, from a monolingual counselor toward a multilingual counselor.

Knowledge

This may be declarative knowledge (knowing that) followed by procedural knowledge (knowing how) (Johnson, 1987, p. 329). Knowledge as used here is the remembering of previously learned material about the culture under study, specifically, cultural knowledge of self in the role of counselor, and knowledge of personal conflict in work with others (Johnson, p. 326). Here the counselor educator and the counseling student can conjointly list mind openers, or questions. To help facilitate making lists, a few words for this objective are offered in formulating questions: define, describe, distinguish, identify, list, and name. A few examples are: List four myths about Mexican Americans. Distinguish between a strong Puerto Rican cultural tradition and that of a

Mexican American. Describe how you would use these cultural traditions in helping a Hispanic in coping with his or her problem.

Additionally, the knowledge objective involves: recalling facts or observations and definitions; thinking; problem solving; and creating. To help in moving from a monolingual counselor toward a multilingual counselor, the students with their facilitator, in concert, can find out where they are along that dimension. For example, this may be done by asking a series of questions about the Spanish language. Words useful in formulating questions are: Who? What? Why? When? Define the following words in Spanish: pain, dreams, work, water, bread. Or list the words you know in Spanish. Or, when would you use the pluperfect tense? If the counseling students are unable to answer the questions or list words, it may be concluded that they are to the far left of the first dimension.

Once the counseling students know about where they are along any of the dimensions, they can decide where they would like to be and use the knowledge objective to get there in a self-directed way. This may be done by: (a) studying Spanish vocabulary; (b) listening to Spanish music; (c) spending time with a Spanish speaker; (d) going to Spanish movies; or (e) listing 10 counseling terms in Spanish that will help to understand a Hispanic client better. After obtaining knowledge of the language, the counseling student can go to the next objective, comprehension.

Comprehension

Comprehension is the ability to grasp meaning. This may be shown by translating material from one form to another, by interpreting material, and by predicting consequences or effects. It means not only being able to repeat or name items discovered in the knowledge objective, but showing an understanding of the meaning of the item. Examples of words used to formulate questions are: compare, conclude, contrast, demonstrate, differentiate, estimate, explain, infer, predict, and interpret. Some examples are: Differentiate between the behavior of a Hispanic and that of a Native American regarding family relationships; Interpret the behavior of an Asian American vis-à-vis that of a Hispanic in reference to body complaints.

Comprehension also refers to a type of understanding or apprehension indicating that the counseling student knows what is being communicated. He or she can make use of the material or ideas being communicated without necessarily relating them to other material or seeing all the implications. This includes: (a) giving descriptions, such as, describe (in Spanish) what you saw at the movie, or what you felt during a counseling session; (b) stating main ideas, namely, read a paragraph in a Spanish journal about two Hispanic clients and state the main idea; (c) comparing, namely, after reading the paragraph in b, state how the two clients are different or alike. After the counseling students are satisfied with comprehension, they may move into the third objective, application.

Application

Application, under this domain, is the ability to use learned material in new situations. Here potential counselors may be placed in a laboratory setting to practice or apply what they have learned under knowledge and comprehension. Namely, counsel a person from a different culture via role play; or counsel a person of different ethnic, sexual, religious, or cultural background than that of the counselor. This may include the application of rules, methods, concepts, laws, and theories about the Hispanic culture and counseling in that particular culture. Words to help formulate questions and mind openers may be: apply, demonstrate, build, develop, plan, choose, solve, and construct.

Some examples are: Apply the information you learned in objective 2 concerning behavior differences between Hispanics and Native Americans in a role play or a simulation. Construct a list of questions that you would use to dispel the four myths that you listed under objective 1.

Application may also include applying techniques and rules to solve problems that may or may not have single correct answers. Example: With the vocabulary learned so far, read several poems in Spanish and classify them into ballads, sonnets, or odes. Or take what was learned under the knowledge and comprehension objectives and apply it to cultural ideas relating to Hispanics. Namely, what are some differences in the Mexican and Puerto Rican cultures? What are some similarities? Apply the same questions to Nicaragua and Bolivia. Or, what are some ecological variables among Hispanics that influence their living, learning, and loving? The answers to these questions would be obtained and written in Spanish. This would help the counseling student to move along the second, third, and fifth dimensions: from a monocultural view toward a multicultural view; from multicultural illiteracy toward multicultural literacy; and from ecological illiteracy toward ecological literacy. Now the counseling student is equipped to apply the fourth objective, analysis.

Analysis

Analysis means the ability to reduce material to its component parts. This may include identifying the parts and their relationships and recognizing the principles involved. Questions may be those that help analyze meanings, distinguish fact from hypothesis, and relate one idea to another. Words that help to formulate questions and objectives are: analyze, categorize, classify, compare, relate, discriminate, and contrast.

Analysis also involves: (a) identifying motives or causes: namely, "Now that we have read *Down These Mean Streets*, why did Piri Thomas write it?" (b) making inferences: "What may we conclude about Hispanic life in those 'mean streets'?" (c) finding evidence to support generalizations: "What does this tell us about the author's attitude about those mean streets or about Hispanics who live in urban America?" "What other evidence can we find to support what Piri Thomas tells us concerning Hispanic life in the barrio?" Answering these questions (in Spanish) helps to move the counseling student along the seventh dimension, from a subjective counselor toward an objective counselor, because it helps to dispel false perceptions about Hispanic life. Or, it helps to move the student away from his or her own perceptions of Hispanic life toward what it really is. Now the counseling student is ready to synthesize or put elements or ideas together to form a whole.

Synthesis

Synthesis is the ability to put parts together to form a new whole. Synthesis stresses creative behavior. Comprehension, application, and analysis also involve the putting together of elements and the construction of meaning, but these tend to be more partial and less complete than synthesis in the magnitude of the task. In synthesis, however, the counselor must draw upon elements from many sources and put these together into a structure or pattern not clearly in existence before. Words for formulating questions and objectives for synthesis are: create, develop, compose, formulate, make up, suggest, propose, design, and invent.

This objective also involves: (a) solving problems: Design an instrument to help gain information on how the ecological variables affect the living, learning, and loving of Hispanics; (b) making predictions: What would we gain by living with a Hispanic family? Or, what would we gain by going to a Hispanic church where services are rendered in Spanish? Suggest ways to help keep Hispanics in school. Synthesis helps in moving the counseling student along the sixth dimension, from a passive counselor toward an active counselor, in that to answer these questions the counseling student has to get up and go to find answers. With knowledge of another culture, comprehension or understanding of that knowledge, and having applied, analyzed, and synthesized it, the counseling student is prepared to evaluate it, which is our sixth and last objective.

Evaluation

Here the counselor is concerned with the ability to judge material for a given purpose. Judgments are based on definite criteria. Questions that may help the counselor and counselor educator are: (a) decide the value of the information gained or developed in the first five objectives; (b) make judgments about the information gained in those objectives. This implies making of judgments about the value, for some purpose, of ideas, works, solutions, methods, or material. These judgments may be qualitative or quantitative, and the criteria may be either those determined by the counseling student or those given to him or her. Words used for questions and objectives may be: choose, evaluate, value, decide, judge, select, defend, and what do you consider?

Summary

By applying the above six objectives in several cultures, the counselor educator and counseling student would be automatically moving from left to right on each dimension. They would also be moving from ignorance toward enlightenment. Specifically, they would move from where they are (little or no useful knowledge of a culture) toward where they would like to be (much useful knowledge of more than one culture).

The yardsticks mentioned above are excellent ways to measure both faculty and counseling student progress on becoming literate and competent in other cultures. Though imprecise, they can give a subjective indication of where learners are along each dimension. Seldom, if ever, is one located to the extreme far right of each dimension. The object is to move from left to right on each, as far as possible.

References

Biehler, R. F. (1974). *Psychology applied to teaching.* (2nd ed.) Boston: Houghton Mifflin.

Herr, E. L. (June, 1989). *Ecological challenges to counseling in a world of cultural and racial diversity.* Paper presented at the 1989 Anglo-American conference titled, "Challenges of Cultural and Racial Diversity in Britain and the United States," Brunel University of West London, London, England.

Ivey, A. E. (1987). Cultural intentionality: The core of effective helping. *Counselor Education and Supervision, 26,* 168–172.

Ivey, A. E., & Simek-Downing, L. (1980). *Counseling and psychotherapy.* Englewood Cliffs, NJ: Prentice-Hall.

Johnson, S. D., Jr. (1987). Knowing that versus knowing how: Toward achieving expertise through multicultural training for counseling. *The Counseling Psychologist, 15*(2), 320–331.

Knowles, M. S. (1980). *The modern practice of adult education, from pedagogy to andragogy.* New York: Adult Education Co.

Ponterotto, J. G., & Casas, M. J. (1987). In search of multicultural competence within counselor education programs. *Journal of Counseling and Development, 65,* 430–434.

Russell, B. (1985). *On education.* London: Unwin Paperbacks.

Watson, A. L. (1983). *Importance of cross-cultural counseling in rehabilitation counseling curricula.* (Report No. CG 020 688). Honolulu: Hawaii University College of Education. (ERIC Document Reproduction No. ED 293 040)

Whitfield, D. (1984). Attitudes and literacy of college instructors and high school seniors regarding the use of microcomputers in education (Doctoral dissertation, University of San Francisco, 1983). *Dissertation Abstracts International, 45,* 49A.

Whitfield, D. (June, 1989). *Understanding and counseling the plateaued.* Paper presented at the 1989 Anglo-American Conference, "Challenges of Cultural and Racial Diversity in Britain and the United States," Brunel University of West London, London, England.

The Effects of Students' Ethnic Background and Counselor Expertness on Students' Perceptions of Counselors

Carlos B. Heredia

Abstract

In this study, the counseling social influence model is tested in terms of whether there are any effects of ethnic background of bilingual (Spanish-English) Colombians and Anglo-American college students. Precounseling information portraying counselors as expert or less expert is tested for its effect on the students' perceptions of counselors. Results showed that the two ethnic groups are sensitive to differences in counselors' level of expertness, but portrayal of the counselor as expert had stronger positive effects, and portrayal of the counselor as less expert had stronger negative effects on Colombians than on Anglo-Americans. Implications for counseling researchers and practitioners are discussed.

Resumen

En este estudio, se pone a prueba el modelo consejero de la influencia social en términos de si hay algunos efectos de antecedentes étnicos de colombianos bilingües (español-inglés) y estudiantes universitarios angloamericanos. Se pone a prueba, por su efecto en las percepciones estudiantiles de los consejeros, información anteconsejadora que representa los consejeros como expertos o menos expertos. Los resultados enseñaron que los dos grupos étnicos son sensibles a las diferencias en el nivel de las pericia de los consejeros; sín embargo, la representación dell/de la consejero/a como menos experto/a tuvo efectos negativos más fuertes en los colombianos que en los angloamericanos. Se discuten las implicaciones para los investigadores y los practicantes consejeros.

Introduction

Strong (1968) postulated that counseling is a process of social influence in which counselors enhance their perceived credibility and increase clients' involvement in counseling before attempting to influence clients therapeutically. It has been suggested, however, that this may be true only when counseling clients from ethnic minority backgrounds, whereas with White middle-class clients "in most cases, the task of counselors may be to maintain an already existing positive stereotype rather than working to enhance clients' perceptions" (Roll, Crowley, & Rappl, 1985, p. 241).

Proponents of the social influence counseling model have postulated that the influence process is reciprocal and mutually reinforcing; involves several stages, which begin before the first counseling session; and that client characteristics such as ethnicity are critical to this process (Strong & Claiborn, 1982; Strong & Matros, 1973). These variables, however, have not been adequately investigated. The limited research that exists about different ethnic groups is based almost exclusively on U.S. research participants, primarily Blacks and Whites, and it is ethnocentric in that this research is conducted in the context of the dominant White middle-class cultural norms (Ahia, 1983; Atkinson, 1983; Atkinson, Morten, & Sue, 1983).

The limited amount of research available about counseling Hispanics (Malgady, Rogler, & Constantino, 1987) focuses primarily on Puerto Ricans (mostly mainlanders), Mexican Americans, and Cuban Americans. Other Hispanic-American subgroups and Hispanic immigrants, which together compose about half of the rapidly increasing number of the estimated 25,000,000 Hispanics living in the United States (Meyers, 1982), have been ignored by counseling researchers and practitioners. Differences and similarities among these groups and in relation to other groups are not known (Padilla, 1974; Rodriguez, 1987).

The existing counseling literature about Hispanics suggests that Hispanics in the United States live in conditions that render them psychologically vulnerable (Abad, Ramos, & Boyce, 1974; Malgady et al., 1987; Rogler, Malgady, Constantino, & Blumenthal, 1987). Factors contributing to this situational psychological vulnerability of U.S. Hispanics include: lack of or inadequate support systems and resources essential for effective functioning and adaptation, societal marginal or alienated living conditions, language barriers, and culture shock.

Despite the living conditions affecting U.S. Hispanics, evidence indicates that Hispanics are underrepresented among those using mental health services, and that those who use such services have among the highest premature termination rates (Abad et al., 1974; "Task Panel Reports," 1978). In relation to this, some investigators have noted that ethnic minorities such as Hispanics may not make the attributions nor empower the counselor role and its occupants as do White middle-class Americans (Roll et al., 1987). Others have noted that Hispanics and other ethnic minorities may have attitudes and perceptions about counselors that must be favorably influenced by pertinent information and evidence of counselor expertness, credibility, and helpfulness before counseling becomes relevant and effective for such clients (Abad et al.; Sue & Zane, 1987).

In relation to Hispanics' perceptions and attitudes about counseling, it is noteworthy that the counseling profession is permeated by the dominant U.S. middle-class cultural value orientations (Schmidt, 1980) that include: individualism, secularism, self-determination, self-fulfillment, intrapsychic and future orientation, and English monolingualism. These values determine expectations about the behavior of clients and perceptions about what constitutes mental health. These orientations are inherent in theories of problem formation and in the mechanisms of change and cure (Strong & Claiborn, 1982). Consequently, counselors set appointments for clients and expect punctuality, expect clients to take the initiative to solve problems and to express verbally—in English—all of their concerns. In contrast, Hispanics tend, for instance, to be predominantly, if not only, Spanish-speaking; to live their lives within the context of an extended family that is patriarchal and hierarchically organized; to somatize emotional-psychological problems; to be crisis-oriented; and to emphasize collectivism, continuity, and cooperation (Abad et al., 1974; Padilla, Ruiz, & Alvarez, 1975).

Available evidence suggests that Hispanic clients' ethnicity and counselors' characteristics may play a determining role in counseling outcome. This points to the need for research that examines these factors. The purpose of this study, then, is to test the hypothesis that bilingual Colombian and Anglo-American college students will give higher ratings to counselors when given precounseling information presenting the couselor as being expert than when given precounseling information presenting the counselor as less expert, and that these differences will be more pronounced for Colombians than for Anglo-Americans.

Method

Sample

Sixty Colombian and 60 Anglo-American community college students participated in the study. Colombians were bilingual (Spanish-English), with Spanish as their primary language, 51 had been in the United States for 10 years or less, and 9 for 15 years or less. Anglo-Americans were Caucasians, English monolingual, born and raised in the United States.

Procedure

Thirty participants from each ethnic group were randomly assigned to receive either "expert" or "less expert" counselor information typescripts. The expert counselor typescript included information introducing the counselor as a doctor with specialized training in academic, career, and personal counseling, and with more than 10 years of experience in college settings. The less expert counselor typescript included information introducing the counselor as one with some training and experience in academic, career, and personal counseling to college students. The manipulated characteristics in the typescripts are consistent with those previously identified in the counseling social influence literature as exemplary of counselor expertness (Corrigan, Dell, Lewis, & Schmidt, 1980; Strong, 1968).

In a manipulation check, the typescripts were rated on a 5-point scale (very inexpert to very expert) by six doctoral-level college counselors, all of whom had more than 16 years of counseling experience. The analysis of the results indicated that the counselors clearly distinguished between expert and less expert counselor portrayals. In no case were less expert counselors rated higher than expert counselors. The mean ratings and standard deviations for expert and less expert counselor portrayals were 4.5 and .55, and 2.5 and .55, respectively. Immediately after the participants received and read the typescripts, they were administered the Counselor Rating Form (CRF; Barak & LaCrosse, 1975). The CRF has become almost a standard measure of social influence research (Dorn, 1984). The CRF consists of 36 bipolar adjectives rated on a 7–point scale, with a hypothetical score range of 36–252. Moderate reliability and validity have been reported for the CRF (Barak & LaCrosse).

Data Analysis

A two-way analysis of variance was conducted to determine the effects of participants' ethnicity and precounseling information about counselor level of expertness on the participants' perceptions of counselors. All tests for significance were conducted at the .05 level. Whenever the interaction effects were found to be significant, the interaction hypothesis was tested by conducting tests of simple main effects (counselor expert vs. less expert precounseling information) within the Colombian and Anglo-American groups.

Results

Counselor Expertness Ratings (CRF)

A two-way analysis of variance for the Counselor Rating Form score in counselor expertness as a function of participants' ethnicity revealed significant main and interaction effects for all factors. Ethnicity (Colombians and Anglo-Americans) accounted for 3% of the variance in the CRF scores $F(1,116) = 5.39$, $p < .0001$.

Analysis of simple main effects indicated that the variance observed in Colombians on the CRF data in the expert and less expert counselor portrayals was more pronounced $F(1,116) = 82.39$, $p < .0001$, than for Anglo-Americans $F(1,116) = 6.49$, $p < .01$.

Discussion

Colombians and Anglo-Americans were found, as hypothesized, to be sensitive to differences in counselors' level of expertness, but expert counselor information had stronger positive effects and less expert counselor information had stronger negative effects on Colombians than on Anglo-Americans. These findings are consistent with those of other researchers indicating that expertness may determine what ultimately happens in counseling (Corrigan et al., 1980), and support the notion that the meaning attached to counselor expertness may vary from one ethnic population to another (Roll et al., 1985). In sum, the findings support the proposition that groups such as Colombians and Anglo-Americans may not have the same perceptions of counselors because of ideological and cultural differences (Abad et al., 1974; Roll et al., 1985; Schmidt, 1980; Sue & Zane, 1987). Counseling effectiveness with all clients, particularly with ethnic minorities such as Colombians, may indeed depend on counselors' ability to establish themselves as credible during all stages of counseling (Rogler et al., 1987; Sue & Zane).

References

Abad, F., Ramos, J., & Boyce, E. (1974). A model for delivery of mental health services to Spanish speaking minorities. *American Journal of Orthopsychiatry, 44,* 584–595.

Ahia, C. M. (1983). Crosscultural Counseling Concerns. *Personnel and Guidance Journal, 62,* 339–341.

Atkinson, D. R. (1983). Ethnic similarity in counseling psychology: A review of research. *Counseling Psychologist, 11*, 79–92.

Atkinson, D. R., Morten, G., & Sue, D. W. (1983). *Counseling American minorities.* Dubuque, IA: Brown.

Barak, A., & LaCrosse, M. B. (1975). Multidimensional perceptions of counselor behavior. *Journal of Counseling Psychology, 22*, 471–476.

Corrigan, D., Dell, D., Lewis, K., & Schmidt, L. (1980). Counseling as a social influence process: A review. *Journal of Counseling Psychology, 27*, 395–441.

Dorn, F. J. (1984). The social influence model: A social psychological approach to counseling. *Personnel and Guidance Journal, 62*, 342–345.

Malgady, R. G., Rogler, L. H., & Constantino, G. (1987). Ethnocultural and linguistic bias in mental health evaluation of Hispanics. *American Psychologist, 42*.

Meyers, R. A. (1982). Education and training: The next decade. *Counseling Psychologist, 10*, 39–44.

Padilla, F. M. (1974). On the nature of Latino ethnicity. *Social Science Quarterly, 66*, 651–664.

Padilla, A. M., Ruiz, A. R., & Alvarez, R. (1975). Community mental health services for the Spanish-speaking surnamed population. *American Psychologist, 30*, 392.

Rodriguez, O. (1987). *Hispanics and human services: Help-seeking in the inner city.* Monograph 4, Hispanic Research Center, Fordham University.

Rogler, H., Malgady, R. G., Constantino, G., & Blumenthal, R. (1987). What does culturally sensitive mental health services mean? The case of Hispanics. *American Psychologist, 42*, 565–570.

Roll, S. A., Crowley, M. A., & Rappl, L. E. (1985, March). Research on client perceptions and expectations. Client perceptions of counselor non-verbal behavior: Re-evaluation. *Counselor Education and Supervision*, pp. 234–243.

Schmidt, L. (1980). Why has the professional practice of psychological counseling developed in the U.S.? In Whiteley & Fretz (Eds.), *The present and future of counseling psychology.*

Strong, S. R. (1968). Counseling: An interpersonal influence process. *Journal of Counseling Psychology, 12*, 215–224.

Strong, S. R., & Claiborn, C. D. (1982). *Change through interaction: Social psychological processes in counseling and psychotherapy.* New York: Wiley/Interscience.

Strong, S. R., & Matros, R. P. (1973). Change process in counseling and psychotherapy. *Journal of Counseling Psychology, 20*, 25–37.

Sue, S., & Zane, N. (1987). The role of culture and cultural techniques in psychotherapy: A critique and reformulation. *American Psychologist, 42*, 37–45.

Task panel reports submitted to the President's Commission on Mental Health. (1978). Vol. 3.

PART IV

SPIRITUALITY

The spiritual dimension is extremely important to many Latino/Hispanic cultures. The strong influence of the Roman Catholic Church brought to the Americas by the Spanish Conquistadores remains a powerful force in the lives of many Latinos/Hispanics. In many Latin cultures, however, Catholicism is mixed with various indigenous religions to create unique forms of worship and personal belief systems. It is difficult to understand the Latino/Hispanic experience without an understanding of the role spirituality plays in the culture. Part 4 of this monograph includes several papers that address the spiritual dimension of counseling with Latino/Hispanic populations. Spiritual dimensions in this context, however, mean more than religious experience. In effect spirituality forms a core of beliefs that significantly influence a person's worldview and life experience. These beliefs have been incorporated in various forms of helping people in need, and in mental health services specifically.

In the plenary paper in part 4, Diana Velazquez articulates her experiences as a curandera working in a mental health center in Colorado. She describes the techniques she uses and how they help the people she serves in colorful detail. Following the plenary paper, Elizabeth Gama and Denise de Jesus discuss their research, conducted in Brazil, that deals with school children's attribution of success or failure to forces beyond their control. Finally, Carlos Tena discusses the influence of Carl Rogers and Teilhard de Chardin on the spiritual development of the new humanity in the modern era of global evolution.

PLENARY ADDRESS

HEALING THE WOUNDED SPIRIT

Diana Velazquez

Abstract

In this presentation the author discusses her personal experiences as a curandera working at the Denver Mental Health Corporation. Specific examples of how spirituality is incorporated into the mental health services provided to Latino/Hispanic clients seeking assistance at the center are given. Also, the relationship of spirituality and mental health in the Latino/Hispanic community, and the interplay between the personal belief system and various forms of mental health care, are highlighted.

Resumen

En esta presentación la autora discute sus experiencias personales como curandera trabajando en la Corporación de Salud Mental de Denver. Se dan ejemplos específicos de como se incorpora la espiritualidad dentro de los servicios de salud mental proveídos a los clientes latinohispánicos que buscan ayuda en el centro. También, se señalan la relación entre la espiritualidad y la salud mental en la comunidad latinohispánica, y la interacción entre el sistema de creencia personal y varias formas de servicios para la salud mental.

Today I have no papers, percentages, percentiles; I have no study groups or control groups. What I will discuss is my experience, and it comes from my heart. I have been working at the Denver Mental Health Corporation for the past 16 years. But as a curandera I have been practicing over 40 years. One of my biggest accomplishments is that tomorrow will be my 35th wedding anniversary. I got married when I was 15. I'll give you time to compute that. My topic today is controversial. Some people think it is a wonderful thing I am doing. Other people believe that I am perpetuating superstition, but whatever you want to believe is fine. What I want you to do is keep an open mind. If you believe in the things I present to you and talk to you about, I think you are wonderful, enlightened, intelligent people, and you are all going to go to heaven. If you do not believe what I have to say, I really couldn't care less. It makes no difference to me. The only thing that I am advocating today is that whether you believe or not does not mean that what I present does not exist. And whether you believe or not does not mean that you have the right to deny it to those for whom it is part of healing. I would like to make clear that I supervise a group of mental health workers, psychologists, and two psychiatrists with my credentials as a folk healer. Being able to incorporate what I have learned with Western psychology in working in a mental health clinic has made for a well-rounded place to help people heal themselves.

We believe that a lot of the problems that we have or that we encounter, mentally and emotionally, come from the lack of spirituality, from the lack of nourishing our spirit. I am not talking specifically about religion or going to church, although that is very important to me as a person. But I am talking about nourishing our spirit. Unfortunately in this day and age, spirituality and religion have very little to do with each other. For our people, especially, the churches really let us down. In the United States, many of the things that were very important to our people are gone—the symbolism, the ritualism, the mysticism. I remember when there was a nun present, you cleaned up your language, and if there was a priest present, you treated him with respect. You no longer know who is a priest and who is a nun because the person who is next to you is cussing like a truck driver, and then it turns out that it is Sister Cecilia. That is devastating because we were used to the ritual and the pomp and the circumstance and the mysticism. We are highly ritualistic and symbolistic people. We have rituals and symbols for everything. We have rituals from the day we are born until the day we die. We celebrate anything and everything. National Pickle Week, National Potato Week, who knows. Whatever it is, we are going to celebrate it because the energy of being with each other is so enjoyable.

At this point I would like to ask how many of you have a concept of what a curandera is. I talk about a curandera because I am a woman. God was good to me and I talk about what I am familiar with. This is what I am commonly known as—a curandera. I don't go around calling myself MEd or MA because with us it is not a title that we give ourselves. In our society today you go to school for many years, you get your degree, you graduate from Righteous 101, and then you hang out your shingle and people will come to you. In our culture it is different. Even before you are born, there are certain signs that happen that decide that this is what you are going to do in your life. The training comes from your family. The knowledge, talent, intuition, or what our people call the power to heal, comes from a higher power which I, myself, choose to call God, but credentials can only come from your community. Only the community can give you the credentials and the right to be called a healer.

Some of the things that a curandera does include laying on of hands, which I use in my practice. We are the carriers, bearers, and designers of rites and rituals. We do a lot of prayers. And I do dispense herbal medication where I work, and any herbal concoction that I give to a patient will be approved and signed off by our psychiatrist. We do massage. Midwife. And just for the sake of not making this a total loss of the morning, I will do exorcism. I always say this to everybody. I don't want you to feel that I am picking on you, but if I do an exorcism for you and you don't pay me, I don't repossess. I just thought you would like to know that. So these are some of the things we do. Somebody that does laying on of hands and herbs may be called a curandera, somebody that does massage and rites and rituals might be called a curandera, in the same way that there are a lot of different doctors: head doctor, foot doctor, hand doctor, back doctor, cardiologist, oncologist. In the same way there are a lot of different curanderas who specialize in many different subjects, and I happen to be a general practitioner; I was trained in all of the different areas.

Among our people we have what is called evil spirits. So clients come into the office with psychosis or depression or whatever and the family is saying they are possessed by an evil spirit. For you that might not make sense. It doesn't exist. But let me put it into a context that you might understand. We call evil spirits jealousy, deceit, hate, bitterness, and laziness. Being lazy, we call that an evil spirit. That one I've got. When you have this inside of you and it grows, it eats at you like a cancer. It colors everything that is around you, and no matter what happens you are no longer in control—it is in control of you. We call this evil spirits. So when patients say that they have evil spirits, I believe that they have evil spirits and this is what I will deal with. We have a new and improved health system. It is holistic. Holistic is in, right? But how holistic are we really? If you have a headache, you go to the doctor and get a percodan. You have a severe headache. You go again and get some demerol. You go again to the emergency room and they give you a shot of valium and a shot of demerol. You go again, and after about the sixth or seventh time you have been to the hospital with this headache, somebody will say to you—a bright, young, new intern, will say—"Mrs. Rodriguez, I believe that there might be something wrong with you." Wow, what a concept. "So we are going to put you in the hospital and we are going see what we can find." After having violated every single orifice in your body, they come back to your bedside and say: "We've got wonderful news for you." What is the wonderful news? "There is nothing wrong with you." Is that wonderful news? But what about my headache? "Oh, there is nothing wrong with you." But I have a headache and I have it right now. "Well I think you need to go over to the mental health clinic."

They do not explain how stressors and pressures, hate and anger, and problems at home can manifest in physical illnesses. By the time people show up at the clinic the first thing they say is: "They think I'm making it up—they think I'm crazy and they sent me here." And then we go on to my favorite part. The mental health status, the evaluation. Can you count backwards from 100 to 1 in series of 7? I always hope to God they can because I'll never know if they are wrong. Many Hispanics don't understand these concepts because they have lived their whole life surrounded by their family, their home, their culture, and this doesn't make sense to them. We had a little old lady, she was about 82, very depressed. I was asked to go to the hospital to do an evaluation. The doctors asked her, "What does it mean to you when we say 'Do not throw stones if you live in a glass house?' " So she thought for a while and she said, "Well, I can't throw stones." They said, "Why not?" She said, "Well I wouldn't have any time; I have to clean all those windows."

I have found that other methods work a whole lot better with people who are not assimilated into the culture. For example, I ask the question: "Are you familiar with God's eyes?" I do this especially for the elderly because the more you ask them to count backwards and what day it is and who is the president and who is the mayor, the more they mistrust you. "You are trying to trick me. What is it that you want to hear?" But what I do is I give them a couple of sticks and some yarn and I have them make me a God's eye. From that I learn about their coordination, their concentration, the flow of their thinking, and even their mood by the colors they use. My office is full of yarns. I take this and interpret it in relation to their mental health status. I think we have 27 little boxes of diagnosis. If you don't fit one, we'll make you fit.

When our clients first come they don't have any problems. "There is nothing wrong with me," they say. How is your marriage? "It is wonderful." Your children? "They are wonderful." Well, why do you think you are having this problem? "It's God's will." And pretty soon they will say, "I've been sick a long time. I don't know what is happening to me. I have been to doctors and hospitals and I've taken a lot of medicine and I have no idea, I just cannot imagine what it could be." So then the clinician will say: Well, do you think it is natural? They will look up and say: "What do you mean?" Well, I mean, is there somebody who hates you enough to do something like this to you? We do have a curandera on staff. It's like, Oh my God, I have died and gone to heaven. We have found that through their being able to identify with a curandera we can cut right down to the nitty gritty of what the problem is. "I feel that so and so put a hex on me," they would say. OK. Why did they put a hex on you? "I don't know. I'm a good person. I never hurt anybody." So then, there is no possible way they can do anything to you because you are not guilty of anything. "Well, maybe I did do something that might have been misinterpreted." Well, like what? "I did have an affair with her husband, but you know, she might have misinterpreted that." So it makes the getting to the treatment so much easier and so much quicker.

Somehow God gave me this intuition, that's what the doctors call it, of being able to sit with a person, and as they are telling me something at the end of the 45 minutes, I stop and say, "You lied to me here, and here, and here." And we go from there and immediately everything comes out. So when you know how to deal with this particular part of the belief system, it is much easier to do a treatment plan.

We believe that if you do not deal with the spiritual aspects of whatever is going on with people, it's not going to work. I believe in giving people tools to work with. I do not like to make them dependent on me, although that would be very easy. It is important that they be part of their own healing. We frequently see somatic clients. For example, I saw the case of a 50-year-old woman whose family had left. All her life she had been busy raising nine kids, being completely involved with them. And all of a sudden they are all gone. She and her husband don't even know each other. After clients have been in and out of the hospital the doctor gets frustrated and sends them over to the mental health clinic or to me. And as I start evaluating them I ask for the family. I don't mean the immediate family, I mean the whole family. And if possible I will go to their home. Because in going to the home you see so much more than what they can tell you. When I am in the home I watch all those people—who is sitting where, and who is doing what.

The first thing they say is, "I've been to the doctor today, he charged me $40.00 and he didn't even touch me." And, "My children are tired of me. They are angry with me because I am sick and I can't find out what is wrong." And of course everybody says "No—we're not angry with you!" So I say, "Wait a minute, Maria, they're not angry at you, they are angry at themselves because they feel so frustrated and so helpless," and it is like their whole face brightens up—"Yes, that is right." So then I give each individual something to do as I watch their position in the family. I will ask the son, whose wife does not want him to do anything with mother, to be involved in the treatment. The husband who is sitting way out in the corner and nobody even bothers to talk to is the one who is in charge of doing the actual laying on of hands. Then the family prays a rosary together or reads the Bible, or whatever they do in their particular religion. Through this comes a union of the family and a definition of goals of who can do what.

Because we are so ritualistic, sometimes one generation does not understand why another generation would do something. In the case of a grandmother who lost a son in Viet Nam, when she feels that the whole world is falling apart she goes to her altar, she lights her candles, she says her prayers, she cries there, and then she goes out and faces the world. The second-generation mother is depending on grandmother to do this but has very little to do for herself. The third generation is very assimilated, they don't need any of this Mexican superstition. Thus, using the ritual that they are most familiar with is very important. I will use Catholic symbols and rituals for people who are Catholic. Water and Bible verses for people who are Baptist. A method for a

Methodist. I will take up an offering if you are a Nazarene. Whatever is going to fulfill you spiritually is what I am going to do. We sometimes tend to look at a client, and although we have learned about identifying clients in our culture, it goes way beyond the immediate family.

One of the first cases I did when I was very young, one I probably wouldn't do today, was a young woman 33 years old who was psychotic and in the state hospital. They were giving her Thorazine and a lot of therapy. They talked to her, and then the time would come for discharge and they started sending her home on passes, a few days at a time. She would then come back agitated. One time she got to go home for a whole week and she came back as psychotic as the first day that she started. This went on for 3 years. The family would go to the hospital and say, "Let us bring in our doctor. She'll take care of her. Let us bring in our doctor." The staff was sick and tired of hearing about this so they said: "What the heck—let's bring in the quack."

When they told me the story, I found out that this woman's husband had left her. She had drifted off into prostitution because that's the only way she knew how to support herself. She felt very guilty, became psychotic, went to the hospital, and had been there for 3 years. So they gave me all this history. Used beautiful words, like "exacerbate." Finally, after listening to all this, they brought her in. She came with her mental health worker and, as she approached me, I started moving back. I said, "Que te pasa Dolores? (What is the matter with you?)" She starts crying. She says she is nothing but a this and that, calling herself all sorts of vile names. The mental health worker took her hand and said: "Now Dolores, we've talked about that, that you are not those things," and I said, "Yes, she is. That is exactly what she is." The look the mental health worker gave me could have killed. The medical director was sitting at the end of the table and he had this look on his face like: "Well, I expected her to blow it, but not so quickly." You know, it's like 3 years of therapy down the drain. But I said, "That is exactly what you are." So I took a piece of paper and a pencil and I said, "What is it that you say you are again, how do you spell that?"—Whore, bitch—wrote them all down, added a few of my own for good measure.

Then I told the staff I would like to use the room again the next Wednesday at 3:00 P.M. because I am going to cure Dolores. I told you I was young. Today I would say no such thing. I would say I will evaluate the situation, I will make a diagnostic impression. Anyway, the doctors agreed on the condition that they would be present. I am sure they were probably thinking that I was going to sacrifice a black chicken or something. Actually I didn't do that because I would have to pay for the mess. But they wanted to be sure that this wouldn't happen. So they were present. They agreed to let me borrow the room. I asked Dolores: "Who in your community do you feel that you have sinned the most against?" "Well, my parents, my children's godparents, my aunt, my comadre." I made a list of these people, found out where they lived, and I said we would be back on Wednesday. I went into the community, knocked on doors and said: "On Wednesday, at 3:00 P.M. we are going to cure Dolores and I want you to come." They said "OK."

When they came, I had stacks and stacks and stacks of newspapers around the room. I asked the staff to bring Dolores in. When she came in, I said: "Kneel there." So she kneeled. I looked at the people and I started stoning this woman with newspaper balls. They looked, and they giggled, and they thought it was funny. Pretty soon, however, they got into it. And they called her the names that she had called herself. And they would look at me and I would say, "Go ahead, just go ahead." They would not stop unless I asked them to, and Dolores would just fold up and she would say:

"No, please stop." I said, "You stay there." "No, please stop." "You stay there." Five minutes, 10 minutes, 15 minutes, 20 minutes, that is a long time. Finally, at the end of 20 minutes the woman stretches out and says, "Forgive me, please, please, forgive me." So I said, "OK, you can stop." I went up and for the first time touched her. Held her, picked her up. I did not say, "I forgive you—go and sin no more." I touched her and I held her and I said: "Everything is going to be fine. And then the others came; nobody said, "I forgive you." What they said was, "My daughter Rosa is getting married on July 15 and we would like you to help us make tamales." "We're having a church bazaar—we'd like for you to come and help us price things."

After that we had a case conference and they told me what I did. They said what I did is called psychodrama. I was so impressed with myself, folks, I couldn't stand it. I had no idea what it meant but I was impressed. Then they said that she had had— I still don't know how to say this word but I like it because it rolls right off your tongue—catharsis. Actually what had happened was that they had been treating this person, and although they took care of the symptom, they were not taking care of where it was coming from. She was doing OK in the hospital, but when she went back to her community, nobody called her a prostitute, nobody put her down, but she could feel the rejection. The community saw her as having done something against God and the culture, but she was being rewarded. Because she was in a state hospital where she had three meals a day, food, and clothing, her community felt that she was being rewarded. However, once they punished her, according to a cultural norm, they were able to forgive her. I always found out that after I punished my kids, I could forgive them a lot easier.

Would you call that common sense? Is there any magic in it at all? Ninety percent of the things I do are based on common sense and a knowledge of the spiritual needs of our people. In another case, I was asked to go consult with the University of Colorado on a child who was 11 years old and was paralyzed. All she could move was one finger. She had been paralyzed a long time. They had even taught her to write and draw with her mouth. I went through her medical history and then all the caregivers who had worked with this child were giving me information. The educator, the social worker, the hypnosis specialist, the psychiatrist, the psychologist—and then they brought her out and I looked at her. A beautiful child. And I said: "Lisa, do you know who I am?" She said, "No, you must be another doctor because I have seen a lot of them." "But somehow," she said, "you are different." I asked for a room and they wanted to videotape it, and I said, "No, we are not here to give a show. I am here to see what I can do for this child." I went in, talked to the child, got a history that nobody else had gotten from her. Did some praying. I have a set of beads that my father-in-law, who was my mentor, made for me. I would pray with the child and rub her body. Because we believe that in working with children the energy should be just right for them, this would be a transformer.

Her psychologist said, "Diana, is there anything that you are going to be able to do for her, any information you can give us on how we can treat her?" I said, "Lisa, would you wave to your doctor." So her hand went back and then she shook the hand with the other hand. The psychologist was so impressed, he was so happy, he cried, he touched her, and he was very, very happy. He didn't care what had happened, how it was done, all he knew is that he had seen some difference. The psychiatrist had to be scraped off the ceiling. The social worker wanted to touch me. But the medical doctor was angry and I couldn't figure out why. So later I went back and talked to him and I said, "Doctor I realize that you studied a lot and spirituality is not something they teach you in medical school. Had it been physical I might not have been able to help her" (I probably would have, but I was in enough trouble already). He said, "What did you do?" I explained to him and he said, "May I see the beads?" and I said, "Yes." I opened my purse, handed him the beads, he looked at them, and then he looked at me and said, "Well, maybe I'll get myself a set of beads and become a curandera." I said, "That's great, I'll get me a scalpel and become a surgeon." He said, "Young lady, it takes more than a scalpel to be a surgeon." I said, "It takes a little more than beads to become a curandera." I think he finally forgave me because he called me in on other cases.

But for the last 16 years I have had to come up with literally a miracle a month to keep my credibility going. If the psychiatrist fails, or the mental health worker fails, they think it's because the client does not want to get well. The client is not invested in the treatment, the client is not cooperating. But if I fail it is like, "What did you do wrong?" But people are scared of me. Sometimes I go up to somebody and say, "I really like your necklace. Why don't you give it to me?"And they say, "Well, I can't give you my necklace because my husband gave it to me." Then somebody says, "Do you know she is a curandera?" "Do you know what could happen if you don't give it to her?" "Well, no." So they give her their conception of what could happen. The minute that person leaves the building he or she already has had this planted in the head; the person is not paying attention, misses the first step, falls, sprains an ankle, and says, "Oh my God, it's already starting." The person gets in the car, doesn't pay attention to the stop sign, passes it, almost hits somebody, and says, "She's really got me." From that moment on, everything the person looks at is negative. So then pretty soon the person comes and says, "Here's the necklace, take whatever it is you have on me off. I don't want it anymore." I say: "OK." I didn't have anything to do with it in the beginning, however.

It is the same thing with our own people. There is what I call psychological hexes. People think you have been to see curanderas and, therefore, you are going to punish them by putting a hex on them. As I said, these are what I call psychological hexes. People get them and all they can see is the negative part of what is going on in their life. They come to me and say, "I've got a hex on me because I passed a stop sign and I nearly got hit and I went up and sprained my ankle." Then we talk to them, we do the rituals, and I'll do the laying on of hands. I have an altar in my office in the Division of Mental Health. We use all these things. After people come to see me, they may fall and sprain their ankle, but when they get up they say: "If I hadn't been to the curandera, I might have broken my leg." When they pass a stop sign and almost get hit, they say, "If I hadn't been to the curandera I might have gotten killed. They might have hit me." Same circumstances, different points of view. If you had told them that it was their own negative thinking, they would have walked out and never come back.

One of the biggest problems we have in counseling with Hispanics is no-shows. They don't show. They have an appointment at 10:00 A.M. this morning and they don't show. Then at 8:00 A.M. the next morning they are in crisis and they want an appointment. So, I say, "If you don't come how do you expect to get well?" But in our way of thinking, we go to the doctor when we are in desperate need. When the herbs don't work any more. When the cleansing with the egg doesn't work any more. When the suppository made out of ivory soap doesn't work any more. Then we go to the doctor. It's the same way with the mental health worker. Clients say, "When I go to see you, all you do is make me cry and get in touch with my feelings, but today I'm not in crisis. I feel OK. Why should I go see you to make me cry?" I think that if we understand this, it makes dealing with this kind of client a lot easier. To make them part of their treatment is also very important. When our clients come in they have to pay a fee. Then they go back to the family and their family says, "You went in for therapy—you went in for treatment—what did they do?" "They talked to me." "They talked to you?" "Yeah, all they did was talk to me and they charged me $25.00." The husband says, "I can charge you $25.00 to talk to you." So they don't come back. But if they come back and you hear their problem and you say, "For this you are going to take a tea, for this you are going to say a prayer, for this you are going to take a bath, for this you are going to light candles," then you give them structure throughout the day. One of my favorites is to tell them they have to walk to the church every other day, light a candle, pray for 15 minutes, and go back home. They cannot drive a car, they cannot take a bus, they have to walk. The nearest church is a mile and a half. And from the exercise they start feeling better a lot quicker. They say: "Boy, she is magic."

If medication is needed, I will advocate medication. And if I get sick, I go to the doctor and say, "Give me a pill." But there are some people who do not respond to medication for one reason or another, and that is when I will give them some herbs. My best clients for herbal medication, for anxiety, and for going to sleep are the psychiatrists. They love that stuff. As I talk about these things across the United States and present the kind of work I do, people have a tendency to say, "Well Diana, you know it's superstition. I hope I never get as superstitious as you people are, knock on wood."

Self-Perceptions of Control Over the Causality of School Performance Among Low-Income Brazilian Students: Can Counseling Reverse the Picture of Powerlessness?

Elizabeth M. P. Gama and Denise M. de Jesus

Abstract

This paper discusses the results of a study regarding the causal attributions of academic failure among low-income elementary school students in Brazil. Data were collected by means of individual interviews and content analysis. Regardless of grade and previous achievement history, the majority of the students attributed their failure to uncontrolable causes. The results suggest a picture of powerlessness—a belief that their failure in school tasks is beyond their power to control. Strategies for counseling in the schools are proposed.

Resumen

Este artículo discute los resultados de un estudio en cuanto a las atribuciones causales del fracaso académico entre los estudiantes de instituto de segunda enseñanza de bajos ingresos en el Brasil. Se coleccionaron los datos por medios de entrevistas individuales y el análisis del contenido. Sin reparar en el grado y la historia del éxito anterior, la mayoría de los estudiantes atribuyó su fracaso a causas fuera de su control. Los resultados sugieren una imagen de impotencia—una creencia que su fracaso en las tareas escolares está fuera de su poder de control. Se proponen estrategias para el consejar en las escuelas.

Introduction

Statistics show that the Brazilian educational system has not been facilitating equality of opportunities for students. The research data consistently reveal high rates of ele-

Author's note. The research discussed in this paper was funded by a grant from the Brazilian National Institute for Educational Research and the Universidade Federal do Espirito Santo, Brazil.

mentary school failure and dropout, and a positive relationship between socioeconomic characteristics and school access and performance, as well as the level and quality of education (Brandao, Baeta, & Rocha, 1983; Cunha, 1979; Gama, Jesus, Carvalho, Lucas, & Salviato, 1985). In general, the poorer the student, the lower his or her performance and the higher the probability of retention in the grade or subsequent dropout from school.

Considering the high rates of school failure and dropout among low-income elementary school students, researchers have been studying the problem from various perspectives. The investigations we and our colleagues have conducted have shown that children with a history of school failure, when compared with equally poor but successful pupils, had lower self-concepts (Jesus & Gama, 1989; Taliuli, 1982), a higher incidence of learned helplessness (Nunes, 1988), and attributed their failure to internal causes more frequently (Taliuli & Gama, 1986).

In a related investigation, the direction of the relationship between school achievement and causal perception of outcome was assessed (Gama & Jesus, 1990). Analysis of the students' causal attributions yielded unexpected results on their perception of control over their performance. This paper will present some of these data and discuss the implications of the results for students' future achievement.

Self-perception of control over the causality of events or outcomes related to us is associated to the perception of having, or not having, the power of influencing these events in a certain direction. This implies a contingency between personal behavior and outcome, the latter dependent upon variations in the first.

Arnkoff and Mahoney (1979) distinguish four related meanings of control. These are: (1) skill, referring to one's internal capabilities; (2) power, meaning one's control over the external world, which can be perceived as residing in the self, in others, or outside of persons; (3) control as regulation, direction, and coordination of choices; and (4) control as restraint. The authors believe that Western culture has built an ideology around the perception of control. They explain:

> This ideology of control is part of our shared theory of social structure. The belief regarding control is that we have control—skill plus power—over much of our lives, especially those aspects that involve relationships with other people and achievement. (p. 159)

Weiner's (1986) attributional theory of achievement motivation proposes that, when confronted with an unexpected outcome (e.g., unexpected academic failure) or when experiencing the nonattainment of a goal (e.g., failure in a test), the person conducts a causal search to determine why this occurred. Research has shown that the various causal ascriptions can be categorized into three causal dimensions: (1) locus (internal or external); (2) stability (stable or unstable); and (3) controllability (controlable or uncontrolable).

The psychological consequences of the causal dimensions are related to expectancy and affect. Causal controllability influences what Weiner calls the social emotions. Internal and controlable causes of failure elicit guilt feelings, whereas internal and uncontrolable causes elicit shame. External causes are not considered to be controlled by the self, even though they may be under the control of others.

A student who perceives her- or himself without control over the causes of her or his school performance will probably put little effort in achieving. Research suggests a relationship between perception of control and school achievement and performance (Findley & Cooper, 1983; Stipek & Weisz, 1981).

Method

The sample in our study consisted of 147 elementary school children, 80 of them with a history of school success and 67 with a history of failure, all of them from very poor social origin. They were randomly selected from grades 1, 3, and 5. The selection of third and fifth graders was stratified according to their academic history. First graders were classified only at the end of the school year, after evaluations had been processed. All subjects were enrolled in two randomly chosen public schools, both located in the urban area.

The students' causal attributions were measured by means of individual interviews. They were asked to mention situations in school in which they did well and others in which they did badly, and to explain why they thought they had succeeded or failed. First graders were interviewed at the beginning of the school year, before they had been exposed to any evaluation, and again at the end of the year, after having been evaluated at least three times. Third and fifth graders were interviewed at the end of the school year only, after at least three evaluations.

The data were analyzed for content by two independent judges, and classified according to the three dimensions proposed by Weiner (1986). In our study, all external causes were also classified as uncontrollable, meaning that they were not under the control of the subject. Whether or not they were under the control of others was not our interest.

Results

The results obtained in each of the dimensions considered are presented in Gama & Jesus (1990). Not all the responses could be classified as causal attributions. In some cases students' cognitions were mere restatements of their performance; in other cases students denied having experienced such situations (27 of the successful students stated that they had never failed); and in a few cases they said they did not know why they had performed in such a way. From a total of 147 interviews, 124 (84.3%) responses were classified as causal attributions to success and 97 (66.0%) as causal attributions to failure.

Overall, about 58.1% of the students were found to believe that their success in school situations was due to uncontrollable causes. However, this type of attribution was significantly more frequent among subjects with a history of failure (73.2%) than among successful students (45.6%), $[X^2(1,N=124)=8.524; p< .01]$. This suggests a relationship between history of school achievement and the causal controllability of the attribution of success.

Because the theoretical framework suggests that causal search is mainly elicited by either an unexpected event or by the nonattainment of a goal, this paper will concentrate its analysis on the causal attributions of failure outcomes. Causal ascriptions to failure due to uncontrollable factors were mentioned by 66.0 % of the subjects regardless of their history of school success or failure, even though these types of attributions were more frequent among failing students.

Analysis of the data by grade level revealed a similar picture. When explaining situations of failure in school, the majority of first graders (69% in pretest and 55.0% in posttest), third graders (71.0%), and fifth graders (67.4%) attributed them to uncontrollable causes. There were no significant differences between the two groups in any of the grades considered, neither did the McNemar test show any significant change from pre- to posttest. Except for the posttest results among first graders, in all other cases the frequency of uncontrolable attributions was higher among failing students.

Discussion and Conclusion

In conclusion, our data showed that students with a history of failure attributed their successful school situations to causes beyond their control, whereas those with a history of success attributed equally successful situations to controlable causes. On the other hand, failure situations were predominantly attributed to uncontrolable causes regardless of the students' overall academic performance.

The above results are similar to those in Taliuli and Gama (1986). Reanalysis of the data showed that about 60% of the sample (185 fourth graders from low SES families) attributed their failure in a Portuguese and a mathematics test to uncontrolable causes, despite their previous academic history.

Considering the consistently high rates of school failure among Brazilian elementary school students from low-income families, these are worrisome results. It is likely that many students believe that they have little control over the outcomes of their academic behavior. Their school success or failure is controlable by someone or something beyond their individual choice, option, or will.

Living in conditions of extreme poverty, often working on the streets, these children are, while at school, like foreigners in a strange culture. They know nothing and they probably feel powerless. What are the implications of such a sad picture of powerlessness for the students' academic life? Does their belief mean they feel powerless in facing the future, in making educational and career decisions?

Weiner has shown that failure attributed to internal uncontrolable causes elicits shame. In our sample, 60.8% of the attributions to failure were internal. Weiner does not suggest which emotions arise in the self in the case of external and uncontrolable causes. But in a world that stresses the ideology of free will, choice, and personal effort in the search for success, failure attributed to external uncontrolable causes must at least elicit shame.

Certainly, the origin of such a problem is most likely situated in living conditions, in the struggle for daily survival that is often below human dignity and makes many of those children believe it is useless to try. But that does not imply an acceptance of socioeconomic determinism. The educational process does possess some autonomy from the social class origin of the pupils and therefore can mediate in the direction of change and growth. To believe otherwise would mean to leave the school with the sole purpose of legitimating an already predetermined social destiny.

To reverse the feeling of lack of contingency between one's behavior and its consequences takes a collective action of school guidance counselors, teachers, and school personnel. If one accepts the assumption that certain attributional patterns are more adaptive and healthier than others, and therefore more facilitative of educational achievement, then change has to be made in the direction of the adoption of better patterns.

There is much evidence that children's achievement behavior following failure can be effectively changed by altering their attributions through reattribution training (Chapin & Dyck, 1976; Craske, 1985; Fowler & Peterson, 1981; Thomas, 1989). It has also been shown that teachers' causal perceptions and their behavior toward students' achievement influence the type of attributional patterns the pupils adopt (Bar-Tal, 1982) and, therefore, any work in the schools must begin with the teachers.

Our research has shown that, when explaining the school failure of low SES students, Brazilian teachers stress mainly the socioeconomic condition of the pupil's family and its consequences in sociopsychological characteristics and readiness to learn (Gama, Lucas, Salviato, Jesus, Carvalho, & Doxsey, 1986). These findings, which were pretty much replicated in a second study, suggested that the teachers believed that social selectivity in schools, represented by high rates of failure, was determined by factors that were external to them and beyond their power to influence. Powerlessness was as evident in their discourse as in the children's attributions.

To promote change, counselors must first work with teachers toward greater awareness of their representations and causal perceptions, and the adoption of more desirable ones. They must begin by understanding that schools do have some autonomy from socioeconomic determinants and can function in the direction of transformation and growth rather than the reproduction and legitimization of social origins.

Next, teachers and counselors can work with children toward reattribution training. Various similar strategies have been suggested—from individualized and group programs to observational vicarious learning. The goal is basically to change the child's cognitions by correcting the maladaptive attributional pattern associated with helplessness and feelings of lack of personal control. Children are encouraged to construe that the cause of their failure is lack of effort (an internal and controlable attribution) and to understand that greater effort makes success more likely.

Given the importance of teacher-student relationships, reattribution training should be conducted by the teacher and in context of instruction and concrete content areas, as Thomas (1989) suggested. The counselors' role would be to consult with teachers in the direction of awareness and change and to assist them in implementating reattribution strategies for the pupils.

References

Arnkoff, D. & Mahoney, J. J. (1979). The role of perceived control in psychopathology. In L. C Perlmuter & R. A. Monty (Eds.), *Choice and perceived control* (pp. 155–174). Hillsdale, NJ: Lawrence Erlbaum Associates.

Bar-Tal, D. (1982). The effects of teachers' behavior on pupils' attributions: A review. In C. Antaki & C. Brewin (Eds.), *Attributions and psychological change* (pp. 177–194). London: Academic Press.

Brandao, Z., Baeta, A. B., & Rocha, A. D. (1983). *Evasao e repetencia no Brasil: A guestao da escola.* [School drop-out and retention in Brazil. The schooling question]. Rio de Janeiro: Achiame.

Chapin, M., & Dyck, D. G. (1976). Persistence in children's reading behavior as a function of length and attribution retraining. *Journal of Abnormal Psychology, 85,* 511–515.

Craske, M. L. (1985). Improving persistence through observational learning and attribution retraining. *British Journal of Educational Psychology, 55,* 138–147.

Cunha, L. A. (1979). *Educacao e desenvolvimento no Brasil* (4th ed.). [Education and development in Brazil]. Rio de Janeiro: Francisco Alves.

Findley, M. J., & Cooper, H. M. (1983). Locus of control and academic achievement: A literature review. *Journal of Personality and Social Psychology, 44,* 419–427.

Fowler, J. W., & Peterson, P. L. (1981). Increasing reading persistence and altering attributional style of learned helpless children. *Journal of Educational Psychology, 73*, 251–260.

Gama, E. M. P., & Jesus, D. M. (1990). *O impacto do fracasso escolar na formacao da percepcao de causalidade e motivacao academica de alunos de classe popular.* [The impact of school failure in the development of causal perception and academic motivation of students from popular social classes]. Vitoria, ES: Casernos de Pesquisa da UFES.

Gama, E. M. P., Jesus, D. M., Carvalho, J., Lucas, L., & Salviato, M. (1985). *O Estado do Espirito Santo: Condicoes demograficas, socio-economicas e educacionais.* [The State of Espirito Santo: Demographic, socio-economic and educational conditions]. Vitoria, ES: Universidade Federal do Espirito Santo.

Gama, E. M. P., Lucas, L., Salviato, M. L., Jesus, D. M., Carvalho, J., & Doxsey, J. (1986). *Teachers' perceptions and opinions about educational problems in their school system.* Paper presented at the 1986 AERA Annual Meeting, San Francisco, CA. ERIC # ED 272.280.

Jesus, D. M., & Gama, E. M. P. (1989). *Ratores socio-psicologicos e desempenho escolar entre alunos de baixa renda.* [Socio-psychological factors and school performance among low income students]. Vitoria, ES: Universidade Federal do Espirito Santo/Programa de Pos-Graduacao em Educacao.

Nunes, A. N. (1988). *Impacto do fracasso escolar no desenvolvimento do desamparo adquirido.* [The impact of school failure in the development of learned helplessness]. Master's thesis. Vitoria, ES: Universidade Federal do Espirito Santo.

Stipek, D. J., & Weisz, J. R. (1981). Perceived control and children's academic achievement: A review and critique of the locus of control research. *Review of Educational Research, 51*, 101–137.

Taliuli, N. (1982). *Atribuicao de causalidade, auto-conceito e desempenho academico: Um estudo com criancas de baixa-renda.* [Causal attribution, self-concept and academic achievement: A study with low income children]. Unpublished master's thesis. Vitoria, ES: Universidade Federal do Espirito Santo.

Taliuli, N., & Gama, E. M. P. (1986). *Causal attribution, self-concept and academic achievement of children from low SES families.* Paper presented at the AERA Annual Meeting, San Francisco, CA. ERIC # ED 273.387.

Thomas, A. (1989). Ability and achievement expectations: Implications of research for classroom practice. *Childhood Education, 65*(4), 235–241.

Weiner, B. (1986). *An attributional theory of motivation and emotion.* New York: Springer.

Impact of the Theories of Carl Rogers and Teilhard de Chardin in Mexico

Carlos Tena

Abstract

This paper argues that the "emerging new person" proposed in the theories of Carl Rogers can best be understood in the context of a world evolutionary-revolutionary process not limited by any one specific culture. Thus, Teilhard de Chardin's notion of the "planetary phase" in human evolution provides the framework for understanding the emerging new person as impelled by a universal formative tendency. The authors suggest that in Latin America, and specifically in Mexico, these concepts are becoming relevant due to the involvement of persons active in transpersonal psychology.

Resumen

Este artículo mantiene que la "nueva persona en vías de desarrollo" propuesta en las teorías de Carl Rogers puede ser mejor comprendida en el contexto de un proceso mundial evolucionario-revolucionario no limitado por cualquier cultura específica. Así, la noción de Teilhard de Chardin de la "fase planetaria" en la evolución humana proporciona un marco para comprender la nueva persona en vías de desarrollo obligada por una tendencia formativa universal. Los autores sugieren que en Latinoamérica, y específicamente en México, estos conceptos están llegando a ser pertinentes debido al enredo de personas activas en la psicología transpersonal.

It seems we are at present at a transitional stage never before experienced in the history of mankind; a stage wherein a number of conceptualizations regarding reality, mankind, and values are changing at a rapid pace. Rogers (1977) realized this and wrote that a "new type of human being is emerging." On the other hand, the French Jesuit Teilhard de Chardin (1963) also spoke about the evident and necessary appearance of a new *human species* that would equip the world with a superior level of self-awareness and that would be the result of a universal evolutionary process. Teilhard foresaw the emergence of a new kind of humanity and culture with similar characteristics to those proposed by Rogers.

However, both thinkers do not limit themselves to the above ideas alone. Rogers (1978) expounded the hypothesis that the self-actualizing tendency is a manifestation of what he calls a "formation tendency," which is part and parcel of the universe, and which moves it toward greater complexity and unity, a formative tendency that makes human beings grow and evolve both as individuals and social beings. In Latin America, and specifically in Mexico, these considerations are starting to become relevant, above all due to the introduction of these very same topics since the 1960s by those involved in transpersonal psychology.

Rogers (1977) wrote that "our culture may already be crossing the threshold of a grand evolutionary-revolutionary process." The term "our culture" may be interpreted in a variety of ways. It may refer to the culture of the United States, which would then limit this evolutionary-revolutionary process to the developed and industrialized Anglo-American world. Another more fitting interpretation could be based on the contributions of Teilhard de Chardin and other writers, particularly those from transpersonal psychology wherein "culture" is to be interpreted as "planetary culture" that includes all social manifestations of mankind. Therefore, we could very well assert that the characteristics of this "emerging new person" as proposed by Rogers are not limited to one culture alone, but are the result of a world evolutionary-revolutionary process, "impelled by a universal formative tendency," and definitely not produced by specific sociopolitical and economic conditions in a particular region of the world.

Nonetheless, this development will have varied manifestations, depending on the geographic and ideological nature where it takes place. It is convenient to remember Teilhard's fundamental philosophical thesis: evolution. Because of this Teilhard proposed that we stop viewing the universe through fixed categories but rather as a dynamic process, that is, cosmogenesis. There is both entropy as well as the law of complexity in this evolutionary-transformational process. That is, there is a constant and greater degree of organization of conscious matter in regards to a greater degree of molecular complexity, which moves from the inorganic to the organic and to consciousness.

Teilhard believes this trend toward complexity is also applicable to the evolution of the human species. He commented thus, ". . . the greater the social and specific growth, the greater the individual and personal consciousness" (Xirau, 1976). This means that univeral evolution pushes the human species to and keeps it submerged into a process of acquiring greater consciousness. That movement of progress and elevation toward consciousness will only end when good conquers and cancels all evil; that is, when mankind or "conscious-history" brings about the kingdom and makes it present to humanity—in other words, when each individual person becomes the image and likeness of its creator.

Teilhard sees this happening quite soon; namely, the entrance into this superior stage of human evolution that he calls "the planetary phase." At this evolutionary stage or phase there will be labor pains and convulsions; but at the same time love will grow both quantitatively and qualitatively. Nonetheless, the necessary condition for the effective attainment of the "planetary phase" is for the human species in its totality to attain the "supraconsciousness" or "ultrareflection" that characterizes the noosphere and last stage of humanization.

In this final stage of humanization, there will be a progressive approximation to the divine energy, and because of it also a progressive unification of thinking humanity into a personalized and loving society, wherein the diverse races and human civilizations will tend to synthesize themselves, constituting thus a totality organically bonded wherein all different spiritual contributions will "converge" (Prieto, 1983).

We are already living this unique moment, although it is utopian at present because it is still a process. What is this "new" person like who is emerging in the last stage of our humanization, and who is already manifesting simultaneously all over the planet earth, including Latin America? Rogers has come to the following conclusions regarding the characteristics of this person:

- A desire for personal authenticity;
- Institutions exist to serve people;
- Indifference for material goods;
- A non-moralistic attitude;
- A desire for intimacy;
- Skepticism regarding science;
- A deeply inner world;
- In equilibrium with nature;
- A person who progresses; and
- Inner authority.

Our world is changing at an impressive rate. The "exact sciences" themselves, with physics in the forefront, are constantly amazed at the elusive nature of said changes, and can only exclaim through their most prestigious representatives that the universe is not what they thought it was. Rather than being a huge machine, it's more like an enormous thought and feeling.

I would like to close this paper with a quote from Rogers (1977):

> If we accept as basic to human life that we all live different realities, if we can see these divergent realities as the most promising sources for learning all of the history of the universe, if we can learn to live together learning from one another without any kind of fear, then we might be witnessing the dawning of a new era. And, possibly the organic senses of mankind may be opening the way for this very special change to take place.

References

Prieto, F. (1983). *Revista de filosofia*. Mexico: UIA.

Rogers, C. (1977). *A way of being*. New York: Penguin Books.

Rogers, C. (1978). *El fennnoureno humano*. Bilbao: Taurus.

Teilhard de Chardin, P. (1963). The formative tendency. *Journal of Humanistic Psychology*.

Xirau, R. (1976). *Antologia*. Mexico: Fondo de Cultura Ecououorica.

CLOSING PLENARY ADDRESS

NONVERBAL ASPECTS OF CROSS-CULTURAL COMMUNICATION

Carmen Judith Nine-Curt

Abstract

In this closing plenary address, the speaker underscores the importance of nonverbal communication to the understanding of cross-cultural communication. Drawing from her experience as an English teacher in Puerto Rico, she illustrates how various gestures have different meanings across cultures. The author also points out how not only gesturing but personal space, touching, organization of groups, dress, artifacts, and other cultural symbols work in synchrony with language to help create a person's cultural identity. She closes with a call for integrating all aspects of self in order to help integrate humanity.

Resumen

En este último discurso plenario la oradora subraya la importancia de la comunicación no verbal a la comprensión de la comunicación entre personas de diferente culturas. Sirviéndose de su experiencia como una maestra de inglés en Puerto Rico, ella ilustra como los varios gestos tienen significados distintos a través de las culturas. La autora también señala como no sólo el acto de hacer gestos sino también el espacio personal, el tacto, la organización de grupos, la compostura, los artefactos, y otros símbolos culturales trabajan en sincronismo con la lengua para ayudar a crear la identidad cultural de una persona. Ella concluye con una llamada para la integración de todos los aspectos del yo para ayudar a integrar la humanidad.

I am pleased to share some of my findings gathered over a period of more than 25 years. It all began in my English classroom at the University of Puerto Rico. I had finished preparing a really good phonetics course for my students so that they could improve their English-speaking skills to the point that they dare talk in the "difficult one," as they call English in Puerto Rico. The work was going on beautifully. It was my doctoral project. The course had been approved because it demonstrated that it could teach my students, who were completely mum regarding English, to talk and speak in English in 3 weeks. They had had English for 12 solid years before coming to the university and they still wouldn't bear to talk. One week after I had been teaching the course, I spoke a bit too fast. And I simply said a very simple little phrase in English:

"OK everybody, now turn to page 23." That was too fast for them. Suddenly, I saw calm come over the classroom and I understood perfectly as a Puerto Rican that they had not understood me.

When Hispanics become too quiet and still and stare at you with big, round eyes, they are not with you. I was going to repeat, and right then and there something happened that really changed my whole life and has changed it for the better in the past 25 years. Suddenly, 10 of my students' noses wiggled a Puerto Rican question at me. This gesture means, "What did you say?" Some of the Puerto Ricans here and some of those from the Caribbean can do it. But not others. I stood without saying a word, looking at what I had just seen. I had been away in New York for 3 years finishing my doctoral work at Columbia University, and I had not seen wiggling noses in New York. My whole life changed right then and there. I had entered, without my knowing it, a field that is practically new for most teachers, not to counselors, not to psychiatrists, but to teachers: the nonverbal aspects of communication. What I had seen was a nonverbal question. No sounds. No noise. Merely movement. I had entered that incredible world that culture teaches through kinetics, which refers to movement and gestures.

Later I discovered that anthropologists believe nonverbal communication makes up two thirds of what we know as culture, and that only one third is language. I have devoted all my life to studying language, grammar, phonetics, vocabulary, and syntax. Intonation is one of my loves. I had devoted all my life to teaching language, and suddenly I found that it is only a third of what I was teaching my students. I decided I was going to find out exactly what the differences are between the two worlds that I touched daily: my own Caribbean and the Anglo world.

Kinetics includes movement, and I have found several gestures from a book that I think many of you would love to read. The book is entitled *Gestures* and was written by an anthropologist by the name of Desmond Morris. He went to the Mediterranean searching for 20 gestures that specific ethnic groups in the United States still use. He found that similar gestures have different meanings in various cultures. That was extraordinarily new for me. In my training as a teacher of English as a Second Language I had not been taught that people communicate otherwise than through language. In other words, in order to understand people you not only have to hear them, you also have to look at them.

Many a culture is so heavily dependent on nonverbal messages that you better look first before you hear. That is obviously the case among Hispanics. We say so much nonverbally. In fact, there is an axiom among anthropologists and other people in communication: You may not speak, but you cannot help but communicate. That I think has been a light in my life regarding my student teaching. But it is not only gestures. In kinetics you also have the smile, and every human being smiles. However, the meaning of a smile depends on where you come from. In Puerto Rico we use a smile among women as a mask to hide deep hurt, deep anger. You may see situations like this: Meeting a colleague of mine at the hospital, "Sonya, what are you doing here?" "Well my Mama is not too well," smile. "No kidding?" "What is wrong with her?" "We had to amputate a leg," smile on her face.

A student would come to see me. "I need to see you, Dr. Nine." "Sure, come right in. Come on. Sit down." Smile on her face. "What is the matter, Sweetie?" Smile on her face. I would then say, "The test?" "Yes, Professor." "Did you flunk it?" "Yes, Professor," smile on her face and two tears running down. You have to learn to intrepret that with Hispanics. That smile is forever there. And it usually hides very strong feelings.

I remember fighting with a good friend of mine who is an Irish priest, and he did something to me that I didn't quite like and I went over to him later and said, "Don't you dare do that to me anymore." But I was saying that with a big, broad smile on my face. "Don't you dare do that any longer to me." He couldn't communicate. He said "Judy, are you angry?" I said, "I could kill you right now," with a big broad smile on my face.

I remember going to Philadelphia once to get some cards printed, and when I entered the shop the salesgirl said the normal verbal ritual, "May I help you?" No smile on her face. And welcoming eyes. Welcoming eyes. I said, "Yes please. I would like to order some cards," but I didn't say it like I have just said it now. I said it with a big broad smile, which is the natural thing at home in Puerto Rico. "Yes please, I would like to have some cards." And I saw her ever so slightly move away from the desk. I got the feeling that kid thought I was nuts. I was so angry that I couldn't communicate too well. The cards were printed wrong, and I couldn't understand what had happened. I froze and I saw that I had this big smile on my face, but she didn't. There was no mirror effect. I couldn't believe that my smile was upsetting her, so I told the story to a friend of mine who works in Brooklyn, teaching kindergarten kids English as a Second Language. She said "Judy, I am going to tell you a story. The first time a native of Brooklyn entered my kindergarten classroom, the children there were all Puerto Rican, and they were smiling at me exactly the same way that you're smiling. And do you know what I thought. Another bunch of morons." I said, no kidding.

As a result, I decided I was going to learn to speak English without smiling. I tell you it is very hard for Caribbeans and for Mexicans to do that. So I would go from shop to shop trying not to smile. And I couldn't. Culture is learned so early that it cannot be changed easily. In fact, anthropologists believe that it is easier to shed your skin than to shed your culture. When I read that, I really marveled at the wonder that one learns so early in life. I was reminded of something that I read while studying for my master's at Columbia. It is a comment on the British and it must have been written by an Irishman because it is very cynical. This is the statement: "The integrity of the British Empire will always be manifested by keeping a stiff upper lip." So I determined to try to speak English with a stiff upper lip. It is the hardest thing to do if you are Hispanic. But I tried it anyway and guess what? I was treated much nicer as I went from shop to shop. Once I entered a nice drugstore with a very cordial man in charge and he said, "May I help you?" And I said, stiff upper lip Judy, "Yes, please, I would like to buy some film." He said, "Anything the matter with your teeth lady?" And then I smiled broadly and I said, "Oh no, I'm perfectly all right." He said, "You're not from here." I said, "You guessed right. I'm from Puerto Rico," and he said, "But your English is so good." And I realized that I had been fully accepted without any hitch. Then I understood something very beautiful which I pass on to my students for use in the first 3 minutes of dealing with a stranger. That is, if that stranger is from the United States, keep a stiff upper lip so that you will have a healthy, sane, face, culturewise, and then shift immediately to your own normal Caribbean smiling face.

It is not only gesturing in combination with language that affects a person's culturalization. Space, touching, organization of groups, dress, artifacts—all of these affect a person's cultural identity. And the wonder of it all is that all of this, together with language, works in syncrony. It's a perfect ballet that children learn and forever know and use in order to feel three things: belonging, identity, and well-being.

Polycronism versus monocronism is another important consideration in defining culture. Polycronism means doing many things in one period of time. Monocronism means doing one thing in one period of time. We Caribbean people, most Hispanic people, Arabic people, Oriental people, many of them are polycronic, circle-oriented. And that can drive anyone who comes from a culture that is linear, where you wait your turn to do things, crazy. Hispanics don't wait their turn because they have permission by their culture to interrupt. That is why it doesn't bother me if you leave suddenly. It's perfectly all right. Yet, Anglos often interpret interruptions from Hispanics as rudeness. I remember at Gimbel's I tried to have an answer from a clerk about a set of beads and I said, "How much are those beads?" What I didn't realize was that I was in New York and she was taking care of another customer. And she said to me seven words. She could have said "twenty dollars"—two words. But she said "Lady would you mind waiting your turn." I was so hurt that I left. And she said, "Where are you going, Madam?" I said "I'll be back, I'll be back." But I never went back until I found out that linear activity is of the essence in most Northern European countries. And here we are Mediterranean folks, Indian folks, African folks, constantly performing everything circle-style, simultaneously.

Before I say anything more I would like to tell you a story of a very wise man who came to Puerto Rico. He was over 80 years old and was there to receive an honorary degree from one of the universities where I have worked. Don Germán Arciniegas, a historian from Columbia, South America, said this, "They tell us we were discovered. Didn't you know we weren't discovered at all, we were covered up by Europe. Why don't we put these 500 years in a little box and take it to the King of Spain in 1992 and devote our next 500 years to finding out who we are?" This is important. It's important to know who you are and how culture affects your values. If you don't know who you are, you can't do anything well.

Another thing that contributes to cultural identity has to do with spirituality. About 14 years ago I was invited by a very old friend of mine to go to a beautiful retreat in the Catholic Church in my home town. The retreat was being sponsored by the Renovacion. I said, "Is that a political party?" She said, "No, it's something new in the Church. It's the caramistic movement." And there I received a lovely spiritual experience. I touched deeply a relationship that I had not known I had. It was with my Father in Heaven. There, for the first time, I felt I was a child, because I was touched by unconditional love. At that moment, I decided I was going to let my hair grow as it originally was. I had been straightening it, because my mother had it straightened from the time I was 7 years old. This hair is low-class in Puerto Rico. It's bad to be African. I decided that I was going to let my hair grow. But I was only able to do that because I realized that I belonged to another culture where I am a princess because I am a child of the Father above. So I decided to let my hair grow out. It was a horror to break through that. But I went to my beauty parlor and I told them I wanted an Afro. My beautician said, "Doctor Nine," she threw the title at me, "an Afro is for the rabble." I said, "Honey, I have a class at 1 P.M. so you better hurry up and cut an Afro, please." And she went over to the other beautician and said, "Did you hear Doctor Nine? She wants an Afro." I was in judgment there, I was on trial, a cultural trial. They all came and surrounded me, and so I insisted I have a class at 1 P.M., so please hurry up, I already was getting ill. I knew what I had gotten into. It was difficult. I was breaking rules. Cultural rules. So she cut my hair, and she finally said as her last judgment, "Doctor Nine, I have done this, but under your responsibility." So I went to my class very sick, very ill, and I entered the classroom and said "good afternoon." Silence. Suddenly, my whole class broke out in applause. They understood that the old teacher was trying to recover some of the dignity that her own beautiful culture had tried to take away from her.

Pope Paul II ratified my feelings and my decision when in 1979 he said, "Christmas is a celebration of all of humanity. Whether you believe in it or not. Because it took a Father to come down from Heaven to remind his children that we were one." One family. When I understood his message, I stopped criticizing North Americans. That's because you don't criticize or hate your own family. I decided that I had a right and a duty to rid my culture of anything that made me feel less a child of the Almighty, a member of the human family. I think it's paying off in tremendous health, and in tremendous youth. I will be 70 in 2 years and I think I'm doing pretty well.

I invite all of you here to cooperate in integrating humanity by integrating yourself, by learning from each other about the good points, the magic that each culture and language has to offer all of us. I think that, like in Greece of old, something very extraordinary is happening in this continent both North and South. For me it's a beautiful, pleasurable experience to be alive at this very moment when the two cultures are meeting constantly. I think that under God we can join in the exciting adventure of shaping a new humankind, under God at that. Thank you.

Recommendations for Action

In addition to the plenary papers and workshop presentations included in the previous sections of this monograph, the Mexico City Conference also provided for discussion groups to interact each day about the content and process of the sessions. As part of this activity, participants were asked to formulate recommendations for action in areas related to the challenges of cultural diversity for counseling. The recommendations in each of the areas of public policy, counseling research, counselor preparation, and counseling practice follow.

Public Policy

- AACD should make a statement to redefine who Americans are now, develop networking systems during this and other conferences, promote studies to reduce stereotyping attitudes based on ethnic differences and racism, and become involved in efforts for social reform to benefit the Latino population.
- AACD should develop educational programs to increase understanding of the cultural background of Hispanics and other people, including their differences and commonalities, as well as the economic benefits of flexibility and open-mindedness required by the global community of the 21st century.
- AACD should develop a statement about the use of divisive vocabulary such as "minority," which no longer applies to Blacks or Hispanics in reference to citizens of the United States.
- AACD should become an advocate for a multicultural perspective in the counseling profession by facilitating training in the field.
- AACD should establish a mechanism that would facilitate international think tanks and roundtable discussions to explore different approaches to counseling multicultural populations.
- AACD should seek the appointment of Hispanic and other cultural groups to governing boards and to other political, social, and community groups.
- AACD should network with different cultural, ethnic, and racial groups in the community.
- AACD should adopt standards for multicultural counseling.
- A coalition of organizations, such as AACD and Partners of the Americas, should support future international conferences focused on Latin America.

- Agencies sponsoring international conferences in developing countries should subsidize registration fees for individuals who cannot afford to attend conferences.
- AACD should continue to foster communication and exchanges between Central and South American countries.
- AACD should be in the forefront of an effort to recognize professional credentials from Latin American countries, as well as recognize and develop methods to identify professional schools and courses.
- AACD should recognize and respect the training of human development specialists and other professionals from Latin American countries.
- AACD should encourage and adopt a position that supports bilingualism and multiculturalism for human service providers.
- AACD should provide simultaneous translation at conferences designed to benefit English and Spanish-speaking persons.
- AACD should make written materials available in both English and Spanish.
- AACD should oppose the English Only movement.
- AACD should develop an educational program on the implications of English Only.
- AACD should encourage its members to be active supporters of bilingual, multilingual education through all levels of schooling for immigrants and English-as-a-Second-Language residents.
- AACD should issue a proactive statement on the limitation and negative effects of using nonvalid, language-biased tests with Hispanics.

Counseling Research

- Studies should be conducted on different types of families and generations of Hispanics from different places in the United States.
- Studies should be conducted on intermarriages, adaptation, and acculturation of Hispanics in the United States.
- Descriptive data are needed on the psychosocial process of migration to determine how differences in goals might affect integration.
- Assessment of the cultural fairness of tests is needed. Assessment of the psycholinguistical implications of different English programs and approaches used with Hispanics should be included.
- Research on the assessment and identification of skills needed to be effective with Hispanic clients should be conducted.
- Studies about the changing roles of men and women within the Hispanic culture should be conducted.
- Studies on the cultural awareness of professionals, particularly those who serve other than their own cultural ethnic groups, are needed.
- Studies on the effect of U.S. socioeconomic policies on the psychosocial makeup of Hispanic families should be conducted.
- AACD should explore new models of counseling Latinos and encourage research on the effects of these models.

- Counselors should utilize available research or conduct their own research about communities in which they live and work in order to obtain data on their cultural and ethnic makeup.
- New research should be conducted in areas such as different models of healing, the effects of different prevention programs, and alternative models for counseling Latin Americans.

Counselor Preparation

- There is a need for more emphasis on bilingualism and cultural awareness in counselor training.
- Nontraditional methods and strategies of intervention with Hispanic populations should be integrated into the curriculum of counseling. Anthropology, linguistics, and religion should also be part of the curriculum.
- The capacity for real empathy and understanding of clients from a different culture needs to be emphasized as a required skill of counseling professionals.
- Experiences of personal shock and loss of control should be integrated into counselor preparation programs.
- There is a need for more experience at the community level and courses or seminars that can provide skills for community rather than individual intervention. Counselor training should include a focus on how to deal with families, ethnic groups, and the community.
- More training is needed on how to do research and intervene in communities so that the value of traditions, rites, rituals, and other forms of behavior important to Hispanics will be recognized and understood.
- Rather than the traditional emphasis on intrapersonal determinants of behavior, there is a need to train counselors on how individual behavior is affected by and in turn affects community behavior.
- Knowledge of a second language should be a requirement for counselor training at the graduate level.
- Counselor education training programs should provide opportunities for living and working in other cultural settings. This can include living with families from other countries as well as counseling in other countries or with people of different cultures.
- Students should be immersed in multicultural experiences. Multicultural counselor training programs should be developed and become known in the field for this specialization.
- Counselor training programs should provide students with experiences that require them to learn theory and practice with an emphasis on multicultural issues. Counselor educators should be in closer contact with the active practice of counseling in cross-cultural settings.
- Courses in counselor education training programs should include the importance of understanding trainees' own cultural identity and that of others. Counselors should receive comprehensive and integrated training that includes knowing themselves and the awareness of other cultures.

- Counseling students should understand the need for change and learn to effect change individually and collectively. Counselor training programs should select students who can be change agents and deal with cultural diversity.

Counseling Practice

- Counselors should make efforts to be nontraditional when counseling ethnically different persons and learn new methods, philosophies, and strategies.
- Counselors should evaluate themselves in terms of their capacity for establishing multicultural relationships with Hispanics and other groups; they should take time to evaluate tests, materials, and standards, taking into account Spanish language proficiency and cultural background information.
- Counselors should take a stance about the appropriateness of professional materials and be ready to defend their recommendations for changes.
- Counselors should be constantly aware of the possibility of cultural transference in the counseling relationship.
- Counselors should be aware of culture and how it can influence them, their clients, and their relationships.
- Counselors should develop programs to help other professionals be aware of cultural issues and the needs of the Hispanic population.
- Bilingual education should include reading, writing, and talking, as well as culture, nonverbal communication, and worldview differences.
- Hispanic parents should be involved in the education of their children. They also need to be empowered and assured that their participation is appreciated. Counselors should help Hispanic parents view education for them and their children as a long-term effort that requires consistent and constant dedication.
- Counselors should identify sources of rewards within the system and the community, and advocate or teach clients how to change those systems.
- Counselors should be culturally sensitive when administering and interpreting educational or psychological tests.
- Counselors should be sensitive to the fact that clients cannot fully and accurately express themselves when speaking in a second language.
- Counselors should help teachers and other professionals become familiar with the cultural issues, values, and traditions that shape the Hispanic community.
- Counselors should encourage their Hispanic clients to celebrate their culture as opposed to losing their culture and diminishing their ethnic lifestyle. Clients should also be encouraged to appreciate other cultures.
- Counselors should get involved in support of actions against the English Only movement. They should make continuing education on this issue a part of their professional commitment.
- Counselors should be professionally and politically active as advocates for their Hispanic clients.

BIOGRAPHIES OF PLENARY SPEAKERS

Martha Menchaca, PhD, received her doctorate in cultural anthropology from Stanford University, Stanford, California. She is currently an assistant professor of anthropology at the University of Texas, Austin, Texas. Dr. Menchaca's teaching experiences include race and ethnicity in American society, Chicano culture, cultural anthropology, and the indigenous heritage of the Mexican American. Her research interests include ethnicity (assimilation/acculturation, ethnic identity, Pan-Indianism, immigrants, society and culture, ethnic group formation, and urban-rural differences), Chicano anthropology (folklore, historical reconstruction, immigration, agribusiness, and Mexican farm workers), and feminist issues (race, class, and immigrant women).

Johnnie H. Miles, EdD, received her doctorate in education from Auburn University in Alabama. She is currently an associate professor of counselor education at Virginia Polytechnic Institute and State University, Blacksburg, Virginia. Dr. Miles has been involved extensively in counseling, teaching, research, consulting, and service. The major theme of her work has been counseling the culturally different, with emphasis on the disadvantaged, Hispanics, Blacks, and women. Her work has led her to consulting and training with government, agencies, business, and industry on issues of cross-cultural communication and cultural sensitivity. She has dedicated most of her professional activities toward improving communication and human relationship skills.

Carmen Judith Nine-Curt, EdD, received her doctorate in education from Columbia University, New York, New York. She is a retired professor from the University of Puerto Rico, where she served as an English-as-a-Second-Language teacher and director of the English department. Throughout her teaching and administrative experiences, Dr. Nine-Curt was very active as a lecturer in Puerto Rico and the United States on the cultural differences between North Americans and Puerto Ricans from a nonverbal perspective. She has written many articles and several books on the subject of cross-cultural communication. Currently, she is a member of the Board of Directors of the National Foundation for the Humanities in Puerto Rico, and is also a lecturer at monthly seminar-retreats on interpersonal communication workshops in San Juan.

Amado M. Padilla, PhD, received his doctorate in experimental psychology from the University of New Mexico, Albuquerque, New Mexico. He is currently professor in the School of Education at Stanford University, Stanford, California. He is also a member of the Stanford University Center for the Study of Families, Children, and Youth. He was previously the director and principal investigator of the Center for Language Education and Research and the Spanish-Speaking Mental Health Research Center, University of California, Los Angeles, California. His current research interests include the social adaptation of immigrants and their children to American society; in addition, he is interested in the teaching of second languages to adolescents and adults. Dr. Padilla has published extensively in numerous areas including bilingualism and Hispanic mental health.

Richard R. Valencia, PhD, received his doctorate in early childhood education from the University of California, Santa Barbara, California. He is currently an associate professor of educational psychology and speech communication at the University of Texas, Austin, Texas. Dr. Valencia's teaching experiences include sociocultural influences on learning, minorities in the schooling process, psychological issues and minority children, psychology of exceptional children, tests and measurements, research methods, and multicultural assessment. His research interests include social and psychological foundations of minority schooling, intellectual and academic development of ethnic minority children, cultural bias in tests, Chicano school failure and success, and teacher testing.

Diana Velazquez, MHW, has worked as a curandera in a Denver mental health clinic for the past 15 years. She is one of the few "spiritual healers" sanctioned by a State Division of Mental Health to practice her art in a structured setting affiliated with a community-based organization. She is currently a team leader and clinical supervisor at a specialty clinic (Centro de las Familias) in Denver, Colorado, and is involved in the development of programs for the Chicano/Mexican population. Mrs. Velazquez has traveled extensively throughout the United States as a consultant to professionals in hospitals and mental health clinics, and has given in-service presentations to university personnel, nurses, social workers, and many others in the helping professions. She believes that culture and its many elements play a significant role in the healing process, and has been instrumental in the development and sustenance of bilingual and bicultural counseling in the state of Colorado.

CONFERENCE PRESENTERS

Models of Self Among Young Men in the Guatemalan Highlands
    Mary M. Brabeck, PhD
    Boston College, Boston, Massachusetts
Culturally Specific Addictions—Counselor Training Programs for Spanish-Speaking
    Cultures
    Roman Coronado-Bogdaniak, MD, and Maria Coronado-Bogdaniak, BA, CSAC
    Montay College, Chicago, Illinois
The Mexican American/Chicano Counselor: Developing a Multicultural Perspective
    Cleopatra M. Estrada, MA
    University of Colorado, Boulder, Colorado
The Importance of the Anthropological Aspects of Counseling in Latin America
    Javier Estrada, PhD, and Margarita Gandia, MA
    Viktor E. Frankl Center for Studies in Logotherapy, San Juan, Puerto Rico
A Needs Assessment of Hispanic Students at a Predominantly White University
    Jairo Fuertes, MA, William E. Sedlacek, PhD, and Franklin D. Westbrook, PhD
    University of Maryland, College Park, Maryland
Self-Perception of Control Over Causality of School Performance Among Low-
    Income Brazilian Students: Can Counseling Reverse the Picture of
    Powerlessness?
    Elizabeth Maria Pinheiro Gama, PhD, and Denise Meyrelles de Jesus, PhD
    Universidad Federal do Espirito Santo, Espirito Santo, Brazil
Support Groups for Hispanic Widowed Persons
    Nadia Garcia-Segura, MA
    Harlandale High School, San Antonio, Texas
An Integrated Theoretical Framework for Drug Abuse Prevention: Cross-Cultural
    Implications for Application and Research
    Gerardo M. Gonzalez, PhD
    University of Florida, Gainesville, Florida
Non-Interpretive Approach to Dreamwork
    Robert Kevin Hennely, MA, MS, JD
    College of Santa Fe, Santa Fe, New Mexico
    Elizabeth Kübler-Ross
    Hospice Training Institute, Santa Fe, New Mexico
The Effects of Students' Ethnic Background and Counselor Expertness on Students'
    Perceptions of Counselors
    Carlos B. Heredia, PhD
    Queensborough Community College, Bayside, New York

Providing Culturally Sensitive Human Development Services for Latin Americans
     Veronica Kaune-Wilde, MA
     La Paz, Bolivia
Latin-Americans and the AIDS Epidemic
     Veronica Kaune-Wilde, MA
     La Paz, Bolivia
Mind, Body, and Culture: Counseling Somatizing Hispanics
     William Martin, PsyD
     St. Joseph Hospital, Flint, Michigan
The Role of the Counselor in Intercultural and Interracial Exchange
     Johnnie H. Miles, PhD
     Virginia Polytechnic Institute and State University, Blacksburg, Virginia
Nonverbal Aspects of Cross-Cultural Communication
     Carmen Judith Nine-Curt, EdD
     University of Puerto Rico, San Juan, Puerto Rico
Myths, Realities, and Implications of the English Only Movement in the United
     States
     Amado M. Padilla, PhD
     Stanford University, Stanford, California
Psychiatric Problems and Culturally Relevant Treatments in a Bi-Lingual and Bi-
     Cultural Area
     Edmundo J. Ruiz, MD
     Laredo, Texas
Involving Counselors in School-Based Curriculum Activities Within a Hispanic
     Culture
     Charles W. Ryan, PhD, and Donna J. Cole, PhD
     Wright State University, Dayton, Ohio
Career Development: A Comparative Cohort Study of Fifteen-Year-Olds in Mexico
     and the United States
     Pedro A. Sanchez, MD
     Universidad Autonoma de Yucatan, Merida, Yucatan, Mexico

     Dorothy T. Soukup, MS
     University of Iowa, Iowa City, Iowa

     Silvia Pech Campos, Mtra.
     Universidad Autonoma de Yucatan, Merida, Yucatan, Mexico
Counseling the Hispanic Bilingual Family
     Daniel T. Sciarra, MA, and Joseph G. Ponterotto, PhD
     Fordham University at Lincoln Center, New York, New York
Impact of Rogers and Teilhard de Chardin's Theories in Mexico
     Carlos Tena, Mtro.
     Universidad Iberoamericana Plantel Santa Fe, Mexico, D.F., Mexico
Demographic Overview of Latino and Mexican-Origin Populations in the United
     States
     Richard R. Valencia, PhD, and Martha Menchaca, PhD
     University of Texas at Austin, Austin, Texas
Healing the Wounded Spirit
     Diana Velazquez, MHW
     Centro de las Familias, Denver, Colorado